LLOYD FERNANDO (1926–2008) was born in Kandy, Sri Lanka. He emigrated to Singapore with his family in 1938.

After obtaining his PhD in Literature in English from The University of Leeds, he served as Professor and Head of the English Department at the University of Malaya from 1967 to 1978. He then took an early retirement at the age of 52 to read Law in London. Fernando was admitted as Advocate and Solicitor of the High Court of Malaya in 1980.

Fernando is best known for his two novels, *Scorpion Orchid* and *Green is the Colour*, which explore issues of identity and cultures in a multi-racial society. For his contribution to the University of Malaya, he was conferred the title of Professor Emeritus in 2005. Fernando passed away in 2008, leaving behind his wife, Marie, two daughters and four grandchildren.

GREEN IS
THE COLOUR

LLOYD FERNANDO

EPIGRAM BOOKS / SINGAPORE

Green is the Colour was first published by
Landmark Books Pte Ltd in 1993

Cover design by Stefany
Cover illustration © 2012 by Cheng Puay Koon

The dedication is requested by the Estate of Lloyd Fernando

Published with the support of

NATIONAL ARTS COUNCIL
SINGAPORE

National Library Board, Singapore
Cataloguing-in-Publication Data

Fernando, Lloyd.
Green is the colour / Lloyd Fernando.
– Singapore : Epigram Books, 2012.
p. cm.
ISBN : 978-981-07-2685-0 (pbk.)

1. Malaysia – Race relations – Fiction. I. Title.

PR9530.9
M823 -- dc23   OCN805344764

10 9 8 7 6 5 4 3 2 1

For Marie

Introduction

IN A TRIBUTE to Lloyd Fernando (1926–2008), following his death in 2008, I wrote:

> Lloyd Fernando was a trailblazer, a pathfinder in Malaysian literature and culture and for his many contributions to English writing in the country, especially during the early years of Malaysia's independence, he should appropriately be dubbed the "founder" and "father-figure" of Malaysian literature in English. ("Lloyd Fernando: A Tribute", 1)

Four years later, as I write this Introduction for a reprint of his second novel, *Green is the Colour* (1993), by Singapore's Epigram Books, I feel that I should begin by re-emphasising Fernando's significance as a literary figure in the tradition of Malaysian literature in English. As a creative writer, Fernando wrote two novels, *Scorpion Orchid* (1976) and *Green is the Colour*, one play, *Scorpion Orchid, the Play* (first staged in 1994 and published in 2003), and a short story, "Surja Singh" (2001). This may not be a long list compared to those of younger writers in the tradition, like K.S. Maniam and Shirley Lim (both who were Fernando's students at University Malaya and were, in a manner of speaking, anointed by him as writers), but Fernando's true significance lies in: (1) his defence of the English language at a time when English was viewed with suspicion and roundly condemned as an instrument of colonisation and a colonial relic; (2) the opportunities he created for the younger writers in the medium by introducing courses in Commonwealth literature and creative writing in his capacity as the first local Professor of English, at the country's only university then, University Malaya; (3) the socio-political circumstances in which he wrote his own works as well as the courage of imagination and vision he showed in addressing the most sensitive and contentious issues of his society, i.e. race, language, religion and gender; finally, (4) his repeated attempts to show, through his creative works, the ideal way forward for Malaysia as a newly independent multicultural society, in finding unity and an integrated national identity in the midst of its ethno-religious-linguistic pluralism and diversity.

When Malaysia became independent in 1957 as the Federation of Malaya, a provision was introduced in its constitution that after ten years Malay, or Bahasa Melayu, would become the country's sole official language. Accordingly, a Language Act was passed in parliament in 1967 making Malay the national language, thus relegating English, the language of colonial administration—but also Fernando's medium of education and creative expression—to the backdrop. However, the real loss of status for English came in the wake of the racial riots of 1969, which shattered all preconceptions about culture and language, and redefined Malaysian society by putting Malay language and culture at the centre. Therefore, when the Malaysian Parliament reconvened in 1971, after a period of emergency rule by the National Operations Council (NOC), further amendments were introduced in the Language Act, making it illegal or seditious to dispute the status of the national language as provided for in Article 152 of the Malaysian Constitution. This effectively reduced English to a 'second' language in the country for good, concomitantly diminishing literature in the language to a secondary role, or what was dubbed by one Malay scholar as *kesusastreaan sukuan*, "sectional literature" (Quayum and Wicks, x), and exalting *Sastera Melayu* or Malay literature, owing to its symbiotic relationship with the language, to the level of national literature.

The year 1971 saw several more actions by the Government to reinforce the status of the Malay people, language and culture in the fabric of national life. The Malaysian society was already stratified at the time of Independence, as the Federation of Malaya Agreement, signed in 1948, recognised Malaya as "the country of the Malays" (*tanah Melayu*) and stipulated certain special rights and privileges for these people to ensure their political primacy. Following the riots, steps were taken to further safeguard this "constitutional contract" and uphold the supremacy of the Malay race (Cheah, 126). The New Economic

Policy (NEP) was introduced to reduce economic disparity between Malays and Chinese and eventually eliminate the correlation between race and economic function (Baker, 336; Andaya and Andaya, 310). Also formulated in 1971 was a policy on National Culture, which maintained that the national culture should be based on the culture of the Malays and other indigenous peoples—of which Islam was an important element—and that it should also include "suitable elements of other cultures" (Cheah, 133). Moreover, a 'Sensitive Issues' Bill was passed in parliament, which prohibited questioning of the "special rights of the Malays" (Cheah, 132).

It was in the midst of such a politically-culturally adverse and divisive environment that Lloyd Fernando embarked on and forged his career as a writer in the English language and as a professor of English. Coincidentally, Fernando became Professor and Head of English at University Malaya the same year that the Language Act was passed, i.e. 1967. That year, too, he launched a new literary magazine, *Tenggara*, to create avenues for young writers in the country. In 1968 Fernando brought out his first edited collection of Malaysian short stories, *Twenty-Two Malaysian Short Stories*, followed by two edited volumes of drama, *New Drama One* and *New Drama Two*, both published in 1972. He also published a second edited collection of short stories, *Malaysian Short Stories*, in 1981. These early anthologies were the first bricks to pave the tradition of English writing in the country, defying the political and cultural *zeitgeist* of the time.

Fernando's first novel, *Scorpion Orchid*, came out in 1976—again, at a time when English was in the doldrums and writers in the language were exposed to the deep futility of pursuing it as a creative medium, forcing many of them to either emigrate (Ee Tiang Hong and Shirley Lim), choose silence (Wong Phui Nam, who stopped writing for over two decades), or cross over to the Malay language (Muhammad Haji Salleh, who quizzically concluded, "Should I lick the hand that strangles my language and culture" [Nor Faridah and Quayum, 124]). Despite this overwhelming crisis, Fernando decided to stay the course and bring out his novel, not so much as a marker of challenge to the country's language policy, but rather out of a simple conviction that a writer is not free to choose his language but must write in one in which he "not only thinks but also feels in the depths of [his] being" (Quayum, "Lloyd Fernando: A Tribute", 2). As a loyal Malaysian citizen, Fernando—actually a Sinhalese from Sri Lanka, who immigrated to British Malaya with his father in 1938, at the age of twelve and made the new place his 'home'—came to master the country's national language, such that he would often choose to give lectures in the classroom, and later, voluntarily argue his cases at court after becoming a lawyer (following his retirement from the university), in the Malay language. Yet English always remained his first language after, to quote from one of his interviews, "I lost fluency in my mother tongue, Sinhala" ("Lloyd Fernando: A Tribute", 2).

Fernando's second novel, *Green is the Colour*, came out in 1993, a lengthy seventeen years after the publication of his first novel. By then, however, the fate of the English language had changed appreciably in the country, as, realising its global, commercial and technological value, the Government of Malaysia had undertaken several pragmatic measures since the mid-1980s to 'reinstate' the language. The renewed fortunes of the English language helped correspondingly to improve the general acceptance and status of the writers in the language; but they remained, and still are, marginalised, as literature in English is still officially a 'sectional literature' and writers pursuing the medium are not considered for any official funding or prizes. Thus, venting his frustration for this discriminatory attitude towards the writers in English (and other minority languages), vis-à-vis Singapore where all writers are treated uniformly, Kee Thuan Chye explains in a cynical tone:

Singapore respects literature in any language by its citizens. By and large, Singapore upholds a meritocratic system. It nominates writers from across the language spectrum for its Cultural Medallion and for the SEA Write Award whereas here in Malaysia, you'd have to be writing in Malay to qualify to become a national Laureate or even be considered for the SEA Write Award, which is actually bestowed by an external body.... It's a case of the writers in Malay waiting their turn to be called. (232)

However, if Malaysia remains a fractured society on the issue of language, it is even more so on the issue of race. Commenting on the caste system in Hinduism which essentially divides and polarises the society, Mahatma Gandhi said that it was the "greatest blot" and "curse" (Wolpert, 310) on Hinduism; "a rotten part or an excrescence" of the religion (Fischer, 41). One may perhaps borrow such expressions to describe the race scenario in Malaysia (although one has to be aware that the Hindu caste system is a far more inflexible and sinister a system and has been there for a much longer period)[1], as its citizens remain divided into two hierarchical groups, 'Bumiputras' (sons of the soil) and 'Pendatangs' (immigrants). Moreover, its political parties are largely race-centred; intermingling of the races is rare and often viewed with suspicion; intermarriage is almost an unthinkable proposition, as any marriage with a Malay (by far the majority group, comprising roughly about sixty per cent of the total population) would also constitutionally require the person to convert to Islam. Thus since inception, having inherited the divide and rule policy of the colonisers, Malaysia has by and large remained a racially segregated society, having many competing 'nations' living within the borders of a single country, rather than attaining its postcolonial goal of 'one country, one nation'.

These are the issues that preoccupy Fernando in his two novels: how to overcome social hierarchy, exclusivity, us/them binarism, and subsequently make Malaysia into a socially inclusive, cohesive, holistic society? How to close the gap between the races and make every citizen feel equally at home, without their having to experience any disparity or undue isolation/inferiority? Again, with regard to the caste system, Gandhi's answer was: "We are all equal.... None are high and none are low.... The distinction between high and low is a blot on Hinduism which we must obliterate" (Fischer, 134). Fernando's answer with regard to the racial stratification in his society is comparable to that of Gandhi; he is propelled by a similar mission of equality, fellowship and justice for all Malayans/Malaysians in his two novels. In the early years of the twentieth century, when Bengal was being battered by communal violence, following its partition by the British in 1905 on religious lines, a female Bengali Muslim writer had the farsightedness and courage to give the following advice to her fellow Indian women, in her essay "Sugrihini" ("The Good Housewife"):

We ought to remember that we are not merely Hindus or Muslims; Parsis or Christians; Bengalis, Madrasis, Marwaris or Punjabis; we are all Indians. We are first Indians, and Muslims or Sikhs afterwards. A good housewife will cultivate this truth in her family. This will gradually eradicate narrow selfishness, hatred and prejudice and turn her home into a shrine; help the members of her family to grow spiritually. (*Rokeya Rachanabali*, 56; my translation)

Fernando cultivates a similar message for Malaysians in *Scorpion Orchid* and *Green is the Colour*—that they should view themselves first and foremost as Malaysians, and only then as Malays, Chinese and Indians, or Muslims, Buddhists, Christians and Hindus. Prioritising their national identity is vital for Malaysians to overcome their narrow selfishness, prejudice and hatred, and to learn to view their cultural diversity as a boon.

The two novels have considerable overlapping concerns in both theme and style; both deal with historical, political and sociological issues, and both are written in the vein of an "imaginative historian" (Saul Bellow's phrase), filtering history through imagination; both are soul searching narratives, in quest of a nation; both are written in a progressive mode, interfused with experimental techniques—but while the first novel is set in Singapore and deals with the explosive riots of the 1950s and the subsequent nation building process in the island state, the second novel is set in the aftermath of the racial riots of 1969 and deals with the social, cultural and political issues in the wake of the traumatic event.

Fernando's focus in his second novel lies on a small group of characters who are familiar with one another and share family or social and professional ties or both. The author shows how their lives and relationships are affected by the political violence in the country and how they react to the events in their personal and interpersonal lives. In Fernando's allegorical narrative, the characters are portrayed as individuals but sometimes they are also made to stand for a group or an ideal. Thus the main characters—Siti Sara, Yun Ming, Omar, Dahlan, Lebai Hanafiah, Panglima and Gita, who are all in search of an optimal country—seem to represent the different races as well as opposing nation-building forces in the country. The characters of Panglima and Omar demonstrate the exclusivist aspirations of ethnic and religious Malaysia respectively, while Dahlan, Lebai Hanafiah, Gita, Siti Sara and Yun Ming, in different forms and degrees, manifest the vision of 'Malaysian Malaysia', or one, united and integrated Malaysia that will do away with racial segregation. Fernando's overwhelming emphasis on the latter view indicates what his solution is for the country's future.

Panglima and Omar are both unilateral and monolithic in their outlook, but while Panglima favours the formation of a hierarchical Malay Malaysia, Omar is in search of an Islamic Malaysia. Panglima believes in forced cultural assimilation. He is of the view that because Malays are the natives of the land, it is incumbent upon the non-Malays to follow the Malay culture. He wants the nation to have a single set of values, and he fights for it tooth-and-nail to the end, to the extent that he becomes brutally ruthless towards all those who stand in his way: he is behind the abduction, torture and death of Dahlan, the kidnapping of Yun Ming and Siti Sara, and the physical assault on Lebai Hanafiah. He also rapes Siti Sara in the penultimate chapter of the novel—all because, as a

Machiavellian, he thinks that the ends justify the means; he must therefore undertake whatever he believes necessary to realise his vision for the nation.

However, it is interesting that although Panglima is a fierce advocate of Malay ethnic nationalism, he himself is not a true Malay. Originally from Rangoon (Burma), he came to Malaya via Thailand in 1941, married a Muslim woman, and converted to Islam. His main advantage is that he has the features of a Malay: "All agreed he had Malay features" (206). It is because of this and his conversion to Islam that he has been accepted into the mainstream Malay community, and through subtle manoeuvrings has become the political secretary to the Home Minister. This goes to show that Malays are not a race but an ethnic conglomerate and that many Malays who enjoy the privileges of the Bumiputra community actually came to Malaya/Malaysia long after the arrival of the Indians and Chinese—a glaring example of injustice inherent in the ideal of an exclusionary Malay nationalism.

Omar, however, is in search of an Islamic Malaysia. He wants to create a "pure society of only believers" (119) and turn Malaysia into "a real country" where all its citizens will be "of the same faith" (53). Omar considers Gita, a friend and colleague of his wife Siti Sara, "a distraction and ultimately a danger" (46), only because she belongs to another faith. He also refuses to sign a petition by his Harvard friend, Sabapathy, for the renovation of a temple, because he does not wish to encourage the spread and survival of beliefs that are contrary to his own; and, when his wife volunteers to sign the petition, he retaliates by abusing her physically and sexually. Omar is of the view that Western modernity is the ultimate threat to Malaysia. Therefore, he leaves Kuala Lumpur to join an Islamic commune and forces his wife, Siti Sara, to give up her lectureship at a local university and accompany him to Jerangau, a remote village, where the movement is based. This is his way of rejecting modern civilisation and affirming an Islamic way of life where the followers will live a modest life of worship and piety (or of otherworldliness) instead of aspiring to 'sinful' worldly success. However, the futility of Omar's aspiration is expressed in the fact that at the time he and his wife reach the village to join the cult, a feud breaks out between rival leaders of the group, splitting the followers into two factions at each others' throats, and signalling the eventual collapse of the entire movement. On the other hand, to be fair to Omar, he abandons his religious mission by the end of the novel and returns to Sayong (Siti Sara's village) in time to rescue Siti Sara from Panglima's sexual assault, knowing fully that "she is not [his] wife" (as Siti Sara had earlier abandoned Omar in Jerangau and returned to Kuala Lumpur, where she carried on with her relationship with Yun Ming), but nevertheless "a human being" (224). This action indicates the restoration of Omar's human identity and human point of view, replacing his former fragmentary identity and monolithic outlook.

In contrast to the polarised and polarising views of Panglima and Omar, Dahlan, Gita, Siti Sara, Yun Ming and Lebai Hanafiah share an inclusivist and encyclopaedic vision for the nation. They all consider that Malaysia should become a composite, mosaic nation where all the races and religions can coexist on equal footing, and every citizen is perceived first and foremost as a human being and, as a Malaysian, above his or her racial and religious identity. In other words, Malaysia, in their view, should be a country for all Malaysians and not predominantly for any one group of people.

Of these characters, Dahlan is certainly the most spirited advocate of unity. He says, "All of us must make amends. Each and every one of us has to make an individual effort. Words are not enough. We must show by individual actions that we will not tolerate bigotry and race hatred" (79). As a personal gesture, he, a Malay Muslim, marries Gita, a Hindu woman, without asking her to convert to Islam. He also stands up for Ti Shung, a Chinese preacher, and Fateema Neelambigai, an Indian-Hindu woman who had converted previously to Islam but is refused burial by the Religious Department after her death, for lack of proper documents of conversion. However, Dahlan's incendiary lectures on unity create violence. He is looking for a quick fix for a problem which requires time to heal. Unity cannot be achieved through destructive excitement or violence of passion, but requires a gradual overcoming of differences through shared memories and understanding of each other's values. Dahlan's death at the end of the novel signifies the author's rejection of a revolutionary method in resolving Malaysia's socio-political problems, in favour of slow evolutionary reforms; to light the house there is no need to set fire to it; to build up something, we need not sacrifice the dykes of prudence and patience.

Perhaps Yun Ming, Siti Sara and Lebai Hanafiah are better role models for change and Malaysian unity. They all think on a wider spectrum and envision a nation built on compromise, consensus and reciprocity; they have the right frame of mind to lead by personal examples, especially at a time when the country is embroiled in an inter-racial crisis.

Yun Ming is a second-generation Chinese-Malaysian[2] who "doggedly maintained a loyalty to his country" (83). Unlike Panglima and Omar, who advocate that non-Malays should "understand us" (Malays), Yun Ming maintains that Malaysians should "understand one another" (82). Moreover, he believes in the "brotherhood of all" (170) and approaches issues from a "human point of view" (170). Even Panglima and Omar acknowledge that he is "sincere" and he "understands." Panglima, his superior in office, explains, "I can trust [Yun Ming] just like our own people" (40). When riots break out in the Malay areas, Yun Ming does not hesitate to carry relief goods on his own, despite the risks. Such gestures are essential in creating trust and inter-cultural understanding among the races.

Siti Sara also believes in cultural reciprocity and inclusivism. She is not a doctrinaire like Panglima or Omar, and rejects their unilateral and monolithic visions for the nation. She regrets, "The colonialists had gone, was the whole business repeating itself? Different groups were scrambling to put their own brands on people. Just like the colonialists…" (122). When Omar complains to Sara that not many non-Malays try to "understand" them, she explains that there are many who do and that Malays should do likewise: "My students, Gita…. Even outside. Many ordinary people show respect and understanding. We should do the same to them" (109). This is her dialogic vision; she believes that only through the spirit of acceptance and sharing between the races can Malaysia positively invigorate race dynamics and develop itself into a plural, peaceful and united nation. Her own plural imagination is reflected in her constant use of the plural pronoun, 'we', in her discourses of the nation: "She developed and clung to the use of the plural personal pronoun because they soothed her: they stirred feelings of patriotism, of love for fellow citizens whether Malay, Chinese, Indian or Eurasian" (97).

However, Siti Sara's father, Lebai Hanafiah, is perhaps Fernando's best role model in the novel for national unity. A Malay and an elderly religious teacher, he bears no spite to those of other races, and even blesses Sara and Yun Ming for a peaceful future together in one of Sara's dreams, knowing full well that there are just too many hurdles in their cross-cultural love relationship. He has no agenda except to propagate the beauty and glory of Islam and ensure the happiness of his family and friends, in particular his only child, Siti Sara. His broad humanitarian outlook is summed up in the following statement, which is also perhaps Fernando's message for building a multicultural nation:

> There are so many who want to force you to follow the right path. Each one's right path is the only one. I am tired of seeing the folly spread in the name of such right paths. I fear those who seek to come between me and love for all humanity. They are the source of hate and destruction. (138)

To find unity in a plural society and to build a polychromic, polycultural nation, one cannot afford to be orthodox or dogmatic towards any one point of view, but rather, must keep oneself open to multiple options, multiple value-systems and multiple ways of thinking, and learn to embrace humanity with open arms, despite the differences in mores and practices. Fernando has successfully embedded this message in his narrative not only through his portrayal of characters such as Yun Ming, Siti Sara and Lebai Hanafiah but also through the cross-ethnic, biracial love relationships between Yun Ming and Siti Sara, and Dahlan and Gita. These relationships signal allegorically the harmonious coming together of the races, notwithstanding the many challenges, threats and hurdles they are likely to encounter, as finding unity in a multiracial, multilingual and multi-religious society is by no means a hasty or facile task; it will require serious, honest and wholesome effort from all groups, over a period of time, to forge a holistic national identity.

Mohammad A. Quayum, August 2012

Mohammad A. Quayum is Professor of English at the International Islamic University Malaysia and Adjunct Professor of English and Creative Writing at Flinders University, Australia. He has published 24 books and numerous articles in the areas of American literature, Bengali literature and Malaysian-Singaporean literature. He is one of the most distinguished literary scholars in Southeast Asia.

NOTES

1 My comparison of caste hierarchy in Hinduism and race stratification in Malaysia is only notional; it is only meant to point to the injustice inherent in both practices. However, having said that, it should be pointed out that there is an element of racism inherent in casteism, as the original Sanskrit word for caste is *varna* or colour, referring to the skin colour of the members of different castes: white for *brahmans*, red for *Kshatriyas*, brown for *vaishyas* and black for *shudras*. When the "wheat-coloured" Aryans first came to India, they reduced the pre-Aryan *dasas* to captivity and kept them in a lowly status only because of their darker skin colour. For further details on the subject, see Wolpert, 24-36.

2 I have deliberately used the term 'Chinese-Malaysian', instead of 'Malaysian Chinese', which is the normative description of the Chinese population in Malaysia, as the former is suggestive of national unity, in which the emphasis lies on the person's national identity rather than one's ethnicity or race as in the case of the latter.

WORKS CITED

Andaya, Barbara Watson and Leonard Y. Andaya. *A History of Malaysia*. Second Edition. UK: Palgrave, 2001.

Baker, Jim. *Crossroads: A Popular History of Malaysia and Singapore*. Kuala Lumpur, Singapore: Times Books International, 1999.

Cheah Boon Kheng. *Malaysia: The Making of a Nation*. Singapore: ISEAS, 2002.

Chye, Kee Thuan. "Kee Thuan Chye". *Peninsular Muse: Interviews with Modern Malaysian and Singaporean Poets, Novelists and Dramatists*. Ed. Mohammad A. Quayum. Oxford, New York: Peter Lang, 2007. 221–34.

Fernando, Lloyd. *Green is the Colour*. Singapore: Epigram Books, 2012.

Fischer, Stanley, ed. *The Essential Gandhi*. New York: Vintage Books, 1962.

Nor Faridah Abdul Manaf and Mohammad A. Quayum. *Colonial to Global: Malaysian Women's Writing in English 1940s–1990s*. Kuala Lumpur: IIUM Press, 2001.

Quayum, Mohammad A. "Lloyd Fernando: A Tribute". *Asiatic* 2.1 (June 2008): 1-9.

Quayum, Mohammad A. and Peter Wicks. *Malaysian Literature in English: A Critical Reader*. Kuala Lumpur: Pearson Education, 2001.

Rokeya Shakawat Hossain. "Sugrihini". *Rokeya Rachanabali*. [The Collected Works Rokeya]. Revised Edition. Ed. Abdul Quadir. Dhaka: The Bangla Academy, 2006.

Wolpert, Stanley. *A New History of India*. Fourth Edition. New York, Oxford: Oxford UP, 1993.

GREEN IS
THE COLOUR

1

ALTHOUGH AFTER A three-day period of relative calm, shooting broke out again in the centre of the city not far from the Campbell Complex, and police road blocks caused a three-hour traffic jam, Panglima assured the organisers of the cultural concert that they need not cancel it.

He told Yun Ming, referring to the participants, "Just make sure they avoid the town area."

That evening in the *dewan*, at the reception prior to the start of the show, Yun Ming noticed that despite many absentees there was still a sizeable crowd of people who had come. He caught sight of Dahlan above the sea of batik shirts, and began edging through the crowd towards him. A girl was talking to Dahlan. She had a wide mouth on which a smile lightly played.

Wan Nurudin, spade-bearded, was holding forth on the *Analects* of Confucius. A group of people stood round him listening respectfully. How could Yun Ming pass by without seeming insolent? Waiters crisscrossed with trays of clinking glasses.

Wan Nurudin was saying, "These are the times when loyalty to the Government is paramount. Even Confucius said that long ago. There's Yun Ming. He knows Confucius better than I do."

Yun Ming stopped, marvelling not for the first time at Wan Nurudin's gall. "Think of a saying on the role of the civil servant. You know—like, 'One is an overseer to all inferiors and a subject to all superiors'".

Dahlan broke the spell cast by Wan Nurudin on his audience. "So who plans? Confucius didn't ask people to surrender their thinking to the brainless." Dahlan was a lawyer with a thinning crop of hair on his head. His pockmarked face, darker then usual for a Malay, made him look older than his years.

"Wait a minute. Let's hear Yun Ming first."

Yun Ming said, "There is something about government in the *Four Books*. There's a saying in *Lun Yu*—'Let the official give himself no respite, and let all his acts be loyal'—is that the kind of thing you want?"

Wan Nurudin beamed. "That's just what I was getting at. Now take Yun Ming, a fine civil servant. But I'm losing him, I have to give him back to the Foreign Ministry. He's going to Bangkok." Wan Nurudin was Secretary-General in the Department of Unity and was used to having persons who listened obsequiously to the views he propounded on all subjects and who did his bidding without question.

Dahlan said again, "So who plans?"

"Why, the leaders, of course. Because they have the confidence of the people."

"Sounds feudal to me." Dahlan's thought came at the hearer like a verbal shaft aimed at resolving muddle.

Sara, the girl he had been talking to, said, "That's what I used to think."

Dahlan nodded. "You don't, now, I suppose. Uh-huh. It's traditional, so it's good."

Sara said, "I mean we've got to use our own ways. We have used other people's way long enough. That's what the seminar was driving at."

"So you passed a number of resolutions and now you are going to force us to observe them."

In the silence that descended on this little semicircle of people the hum of conversation in the hall suddenly sounded louder.

Wan Nurudin stroked his beard. "What we have formed are guidelines," he said. He returned ostentatiously away from Dahlan to address his more docile listeners. "That's the trouble with some people today. Everything we do they measure by Western criteria. When I was—"

A waiter thrust a tray of tidbits at them. Wan Nurudin's hearers reached at the tray in reflex fashion, and he raised his voice to retain their attention. Yun Ming pulled Dahlan away and said, "Hey, Dahlan."

Dahlan said, "Ay, man!" But his look contradicted the familiarity of the greeting.

Yun Ming's smile froze as he thought how easily the memory of old friendship could be repulsed. As freshmen they had, at the behest of their seniors, waded or crawled across the muddy Bukit Timah canal between their residential hall and the University grounds. They had sat on low, wooden stools and drunk *teh halia*—ginger tea—at Wahab's stall at three in the morning, arguing about the view that the Chinese were the Jews of Asia, and about Eurocentric biases in social theories about the Malays. Meeting now for the first time so many years later, Dahlan's gaze had only polite, wary attention. Maybe time was needed to wear out stiffness. But then again, maybe time was the culprit which had changed them both so much. There was nothing for it but to get to the point.

Yun Ming said, "Do me a favour."

Dahlan stared at him.

Yun Ming said, "You're already in trouble, don't make things worse."

"What do you mean?"

"Why talk back to the Secretary-General? Let him talk, why make him angry?" Dahlan shook his head in an exaggerated gesture of despair. "Ay, I heard you were working that guy's Ministry. But you're really gone man, I didn't know how far."

"When you go for the interview—"

Dahlan said, "I went last week. You don't know ah?"

Yun Ming did not know. He said impassively, "I'm talking about the next one."

Dahlan laughed with mock heartiness. "You did not know about the first one. Why should there be another one? There won't be another." He turned to Sara. "Let me introduce you to Yun Ming. He's a very important man. He arranges interviews for me. Don't want the interviews also cannot. Must go." A delegate who had been standing nearby with a glass in hand and a fixed smile on his face, laughed uncertainly. "This is Siti Sara Hanafiah."

Yun Ming glanced briefly at the girl and said, "Hullo." She smiled. Her gaze disconcerted him.

"She studied Sociology in the States. She's a lecturer in the University. You know Omar? Ministry of Trade? His wife. He's not here tonight."

"He's gone outstation," she murmured as she shook hands.

Yun Ming drew him aside. "Dahlan, listen I can't stop. When you go again, it's just a normal requirement—just a form. Just say the words. They've really got nothing against you. They just don't want to make exceptions. They know you, you see."

"I see." Dahlan mocked him. "You think you are so great, anything you say I must jump." His forced laughter was irritating. "Here, Sara, come here." She approached wide-eyed. "Let me tell you more about this guy." He turned to Yun Ming. "You don't mind if I call you 'this guy'? We've been friends for so long, what. You're a nice fellow. You're sincere. You work hard for that guy," he jerked his head sideways in the direction of Wan Nurudin, "and that guy" he nodded at Panglima and then spoke directly to Sara. "Trouble is he doesn't know—doesn't want to know what bastards those guys are."

Yun Ming's face was mottled. "I don't have much time left. That's why I'm talking to you."

"Yeah, I heard just now. Bangkok, eh? Have a nice time with the girls." Dahlan had a glint in his eyes: he wanted to make Yun Ming uncomfortable in the presence of the girl. "You think your posting is a reward? They only want you out of the way, man. You didn't know about my first interview, now did you? See what I mean?"

"I'm trying to say something to you. Do you understand?"

"No need. You know the kind of buggers you're working for and you still work for them. And see what they do to you."

Yun Ming said, "My God, man, don't you know the trouble that's going on outside?"

Dahlan said, "Okay. Do you know the root causes of the trouble? You want to argue with me, okay, I'll argue with you."

Yun Ming turned away. Nobody could say he had not tried.

At the bar he met Panglima sipping orange cordial. "I know, Ming," Panglima said, his lips hardly moving. "I saw what happened. Now we must keep him from the Minister." Panglima had a square, balding head, and behind thick glasses—eyes that narrowed as if by habit. When Yun Ming looked questioningly at him, he said, "Don't worry, I've arranged for that. Take a look."

The Minister of Culture was at that moment laughing heartily at something he himself had said. The Yang di-Pertua remained expressionless. He picked a skewer of *satay* from a dish held out to him and dipped it in the bowl of peanut sauce. A circle of men stood round the two like a casual barrier.

Panglima said, "See those men. Ours."

"How do you know he wants to see the Minister?"

"He's been phoning the Suria Complex for more than a week now trying to get an appointment. We blocked him. He knows he's in trouble. He has to work fast." Dahlan was banking on old friendship with the Minister. They had been law students together in London. He might succeed. If he got through. Tonight may be his only chance, Panglima said. His eyes were mere slits as he watched intently. Suddenly he said, "He's got through!"

Dahlan had barged through the discreet barrier and was now shaking hands with the Minister. They began an earnest conversation.

But it did not last long. A moment later Wan Nurudin had insinuated himself between them, and Dahlan's chance was gone. The Minister and the Yang di-Pertua were hastily led by Wan Nurudin into the auditorium, their aides straggling obsequiously behind.

Dahlan stood nonplussed. His head jerked from side to side as if he was looking for something or someone. He caught sight of Panglima looking at him with a faintly mocking smile.

He turned and walked away stiffly. There was no one in this gathering who would offer him help. Sara could not. She did not understand what had happened. She was laughing and chatting with some of the guests as they moved slowly towards the entrance to the auditorium. She called out to him as he passed by, "The show is starting," but his face was set and he did not seem to hear. He went up to the bar and ordered a drink.

Yun Ming said, "Aren't you going in?"

Dahlan turned and glowered at him. "Did you see that?"

The other stared steadily at him.

Dahlan said, "I said did you see that?"

"What did you expect?"

Dahlan was trembling. "Screw you."

Sara come back and said, "You better go in now, the show is starting." She fumbled with her handbag briefly, glancing from one to the other as she did so. "Is anything the matter?" Neither looked at her. "I'm sorry, I don't want to interrupt you. But I want to ask a favour and—"

Yun Ming said, "I only want to say—"

"Yeah. Never mind."

"You think you're so special; who the hell are you, man? You just come to these functions and expect us to say how great you are simply because you criticise everything. You want to talk like those fellows in Hyde Park, you better go back to London."

Dahlan said, "I know the way you want me to talk. You told me just now. Now tell me something else. Why are you doing this? Being so kind, want to advise me. I tell you now it's no use man, you hear? No use. In spite of what happened just now. I don't know why you joined those buggers. That bloody Janggut is a shit. All of you are shits. Why, because you all want to do this to us." He made a gesture with his fist. "Do me a favour man, ay? Just go back to Janggut and do what you're good at. Carry his balls."

"Harry, this is not the university any more. When we were there you talked like this, nothing happened. What I'm telling you is now, man, now. If you carry on like you've been doing, see what happens. I'm trying to tell you you've gone too far."

"What happens to me, never mind. What's happened to you ah, tell me that. I still cannot believe it. You. You have become—" Dahlan waved a hand in disgust. "Ah—h-h—you make me sick." He put his glass on the bar and strode away. Then he stopped and turned around. "I have another saying from Confucius. Confucius, he say, 'Those who lick arse shall be shat upon'."

Yun Ming, trembling, stared after Dahlan for a long time. He thought: He's determined to be juvenile. It was easy for him to talk. Just attack everything. Just like the *mat sallehs*. Everything they want to say about us, you say for them. No need for them to say anything. Dahlan will speak. Just criticise everything we do. Dahlan was going on as if there had never been any change. There was no originality in him. He was just an imitation radical. A colonial product to the end.

An apprehension that someone was watching him made him turn involuntarily. Sara was still standing as if she were waiting for permission to speak. In the dimmed lighting of the concourse the light fixture on the pillar near which she stood shone like a flare. She looked golden in the light which fell upon her face.

He stared at her and said, "I'm sorry", although he did not know what he was apologising for.

She said, "Hope you don't mind if I ask you a favour? You're Dahlan's friend, no? Even though you were quarrelling? You were quarrelling?"

He nodded ruefully. He was looking at her but he did not seem to be listening.

"Can you give me a lift?" she asked. "You see I came with Panglima because my husband is outstation. Panglima is from my hometown. Trouble is—"

The eyes were large with curling lashes, the lips full and sensuous, her complexion, though she now no longer stood near pillar, still golden. She wore a *baju kurung* which glistened in the dim light.

He said, "What did you say?"

"I said—"

"Yah, you want a lift. It's okay. I'll take you home after the show." He broke off, feeling unseen eyes studying them. "You want to leave before the end?"

"Yes. Before Panglima finds out. I'll explain why."

Yun Ming said, "No need. Say, ten-thirty?"

The concourse had thinned out and still she remained. He could not make her out. There was no shadow in her face, her eyes were wide open now like a child's and looked at him frankly, and her words flowed in a running stream. For a moment Yun Ming felt they were enclosed in the real world from which the shadow world had been excluded.

From inside the hall came the melodious clanging of the *gamelan*. The vigorous beat of the music was wafted to them in waves. They listened in unconscious unison, delighted by the jangling symphony of sounds until they became aware of curious glances of the hall attendants cast in their direction. Yun Ming turned abruptly and walked away saying, "I'll meet you here at ten-thirty."

2

THEY DROVE AWAY from the *dewan* unnoticed. Yun Ming waited on the outer steps standing as if he were looking intently at a neon advertisement which blinked on and off in an irregular pattern. She caught sight of his stocky frame and he gave her a brief glance before he led the way to his car. He drove slowly, even reflectively out of the suburb onto the highway leading into the city, before she told him where she wanted to be dropped.

He said, "Is that on the other side of the railway tracks?"

"Yes. But I can get off just before the bridge and walk across."

He said he would take her right up to her house. She did not protest. They spoke perfunctorily about the Dance Company's performance that evening. Then she said, "Let me explain about tonight. I mean why I asked for a lift."

She had come with Panglima and his wife. Panglima was from her own *kampung*, and a friend of her father's. The trouble was, she laughed self-consciously, she was embarrassed to return with him.

"Why?" He drove slowly, allowing other cars to roar past.

"You know him."

"Yes. He's my boss. Was he trying to get smart with you?"

"Maybe I shouldn't say anything more."

He took his eye off the road to look at her as he said, "It doesn't matter. I am glad to give you a lift."

They were silent for a while. Then she said, "When we were coming to the show, he picked me up first, then he drove to a quiet spot and tried to get fresh. I wouldn't let him, so he's in a rage. When he went back to pick up Hasnah—his wife—he told her to sit in the back seat of the car, and he asked me to sit in front with him."

Thinking of what she had said earlier, he said, "You're from Perak."

"Sayong is your *kampung* then. Panglima is from there. There is an agriculture station there. I've been there a few times myself."

"Where are you from?"

"Just Kuala Lumpur," he said with mock apology. His manner disarmed her.

She said, "I have been away too long. Things have changed a lot. People too. My father contacted Panglima since he's from my hometown and asked him to keep in touch with me. You know he's something of a big shot. Actually he was quite helpful to us—me and my husband, I mean. Especially when we came back from the States. He knows people. We got a telephone fast. We got a car and a fridge on easy payments, no deposit—that kind of things."

Near the turn-off at Angkasapuri, he stepped suddenly on

the brakes, jerking her forward. Three or four torchlights flashed wildly at him from the dark road ahead like glow-worms.

He said, "Put your window up and lock your door."

The cars in front of him had slowed down. Now they came to a dead stop. The street lights were out and the metal of the vehicles arrested ahead on the darkened road shone dully. A figure came up to Yun Ming's side of the car and tapped on the glass, gesticulating as he did so. After a few seconds' hesitation Yun Ming wound down his window a bit.

The figure said in Cantonese, "Indians are attacking shops. Near the rail crossing. What for, don't know." The figure bent lower, angling his head as he peered into the car and stared at Sara. "She's Chinese or Malay? Malay not safe, you know. She's Malay, better you wait a while, let other car go first."

Yun Ming said, "What about Campbell Road?"

The man said it was okay, the soldiers were there. Now there was trouble in Ipoh Road. Not Indians. Some other group.

Yun Ming edged his car to the side of the road and switched off his engine. Other cars had done likewise. A few moved on. They watched as figures dashed past, some shouting. More cars pulled up behind them until the road was fully packed.

He said, "Nothing to do but wait."

He could see she was frightened but was trying not to show it. Later on he thought about the things they talked about while waiting. The Seminar, the speakers, the Communists, the fundamentalists, Dahlan. The occasional flurry of footsteps ceased to alarm or even distract them. She told him she had known Dahlan since their sixth form days in Ipoh. They had belonged to the school's drama club and had acted in plays together. She had once been Rosalind, he Jacques.

"You know what he's doing now?" he asked.

"He's a lawyer, yes. Oh you mean politically."

"Yes."

"He's quite frank, that I know. Even in school he spoke out." She broke off. "I don't fully know what's been going on. I know he still speaks his mind. Like tonight. Is that what you mean?"

"Not just that."

"I hear he's spoken at rallies. Very strongly. He's roused up feelings, they say."

She was provoking him now, Yun Ming thought. He said, "Some people love to hear him. Others hate his guts. He talks about racial matters, religion—have you heard him speak on religion? That seminar some months ago, were you here? My God, he really made people angry."

She said, "Those who don't know him can easily misunderstand him."

"Enough to want to hurt him. He's in trouble and he doesn't seem to care. Maybe you can help him."

She asked politely, "What were you quarrelling about? You don't think—"

He said, "You know what he's done? I don't mean just, what you call, speaking his mind. That we can take but—"

"We," she repeated his word thoughtfully.

He stuttered a little and then said shortly, "All right. I don't want to get into an argument with you. If you're his friend talk to him."

"About what?"

Was she trying to be difficult? Play deadpan, don't answer, use the Socratic method of questioning even for the most obvious facts. He said, "I suppose you will say it's nothing very much."

"You're also his friend, no? Have you talked to him?"

He tried to keep the irritation out of his voice. "You saw what happened at the *dewan*, didn't you."

"What has he done?"

He searched for the words for a few moments, and when they occurred to him, he thought she would say: what a thing to complain of. He supposed it was a great thing to be able to do what Dahlan did and was doing. The pseudo-intellectuals would gather around him and admire his active commitment. It was in the best traditions of liberalism. If he was arrested, they would pass the hat round for his defence. If there was no trial they would murmur in the luxury of their living rooms at night. None of them would look any further to ask, Are not Dahlan's opponents committed, too? Is not Dahlan wrong just to bring an idea in without asking how it should be brought in for people of different cultures?

He took a deep breath and said, "Three weeks ago he stood on the steps of St. Peter's Church in Malacca and made some remarks about religious intolerance. Just himself. He didn't announce it in advance. A few people stopped to listen to him—maybe I should say, to watch him. Now he says he wants to do it again."

"And that's the problem."

"There was a fight among some youths that evening near the church. What with the disturbances that have begun, he's not making things better, he's only making them worse. If he really means to carry on like that—" he stopped as if he had completed his sentence.

They listened to the barking of dogs from the houses nearby. In the distance heavy vehicles were passing along the other highway. On their road some cars were starting up and even in the cool of the night the exhaust fumes made Yun Ming's head spin.

A voice shouted, "Cheh! Don't know how to pray, cannot let other people pray also. Next time you better look out, I put some shit in your place. Then only you will know." Several other voices were raised in reply, the ground shook slightly as scurrying feet padded along the moonlit grass verge. Then the cars began to move again, some untidily edging into the right-hand lane and edging back when it did not move fast enough.

He felt vaguely dissatisfied. She did not understand the urgency. Then again, maybe she didn't mean to be sceptical, maybe it just a manner picked up from her university overseas. Even when she was talking seriously the manner could not dampen her beguiling impulsiveness. Like when she asked him for a lift.

They were now on Jalan Bangsar, the traffic from both directions moving slowly and without hindrance. At the railway crossing the road glistened with splintered glass. Two cars stood parked, their bodies dented, their bonnets and boot-lids raised high. In a neon-lit coffeeshop nearby a man sat with his head bandaged while three shirtless urchins stood round him looking at him curiously. People from the shanty houses below the verge on the other side of the road had come out and now stood in groups, *sarong*-clad, arms folded, staring at a scene from which the main actors had departed.

They crossed the bridge over the railway line, went round what passed for a roundabout and stopped just past a large, gloomy angsana tree.

They had been silent for this last part of the journey. She said, "Thanks", and steadfastly refused his offer to accompany her along a short, dark stretch of the lane to her house.

He said, "It's dangerous. I'd better accompany you."

She opened the car door on her side, turned back to him and smiled. Then she was gone.

For the next few days, Yun Ming avoided Panglima's telephone calls. He was caught once; Panglima was at the other end. Yun Ming mumbled something about a meeting in the Secretary-General's office and hastily put down the receiver. Then he thought it might be a good idea to meet him, to scrutinise once again the visage of the man who was his guide and immediate superior. What would he find there that he would not find in the faces of other men, including his own?

"Ming ah. Ay, why your face so sour like that?" It was Tengku. She really was a Tengku—Tengku Sabariah in fact. She was his office assistant.

Yun Ming said, "Yah what. You don't finish your work who gets the blame? I get the blame."

She wore expensive clothes over her slight, small frame. She often repainted her lips in the office outside Yun Ming's room, where the general staff worked, re-rouged her fair cheeks, adjusted and re-adjusted her bangles and rings from time to time, and smiled with a sweetly vacant look at each and every visitor to the office. The rest of the staff had long since ceased to take any notice of her save to say, "Tengku, do this list", or "Tengku, this one got mistakes, do again", and she would, with the same sweetly vacant look, attend to the task given to her for a few minutes before she got up and wandered off. She liked Yun Ming because he didn't scold her. He always explained things nicely. At one time she thought he was 'interested' in her, as she told her brother, but nothing happened. She sometimes took advantage of her status to make a mild bantering remark to him and he would reply in kind.

She smiled through her heavy makeup. "So many days you're looking serious, come near you also, I'm scared."

"Got work lah, Tengku."

"I think so you have a friend. Am I right?" She did not stop for an answer. "See? I know I am right."

Yun Ming went into his room and picked up the telephone. This time he got through to Sara.

"Oh it's you," she said. "I thought it was the Ministry—"

"Yeah, it's where I work. I called many times but you were giving lectures or something."

"Sorry. Well—how are you? Oh thank you for giving me a lift that night."

His mind had suddenly gone blank, and there was silence on the line for a while.

"Hullo?"

"Hullo?"

At last he said, "What did you tell Panglima?"

She laughed. "I called the next day and I said I had a bad stomachache and had to rush home."

"About—about—our friend. You know who I mean? I wanted to explain a little bit more."

She came in hastily. "It's okay, there's no need. I've spoken to him. He's told me everything."

She spoke urgently. He said it was important she knew why Dahlan might be in trouble. They met outside the Federal Cinema and walked to a *nasi padang* shop on Jalan Chow Kit.

"He could be taken in," he said, when they sat down at a marble-topped table after ordering some food.

She stated at him. "Why?"

"It's no use asking why. You've been away too long. You will understand by and by."

A girl came up and cleared away from the marble top bits of chewed-up chicken bones, spilt soya sauce, and scattered rice grains with a soiled rag. They moved their plastic stools closer to make room for three smartly-dressed office girls who were shown to their table. It was lunchtime, and the shop was crowded. Above the noise of the passing traffic on the street outside, the girl attendant shouted an order to the man at the front of the shop where steamed and roasted chickens hung by their throats on short, iron hooks. An Indian man in a thin, white *dhoti* held out some lottery tickets spread out in a fan, like a hand of cards. He held this posture for a few seconds and when they did not take any notice, moved to the next table.

Their food arrived and they commenced eating. The *rendang* sat in a dark, velvet brown gravy against a background of crimson oil. He scooped up a piece with his spoon and fork and put it in her plate. Then he helped himself. It was when he was about to put a spoonful of rice and curried chicken into his mouth that he caught sight of the man gazing at him with a fixed stare as he picked his teeth. The jaws were open at a distorted angle, the thumb and forefinger holding the toothpick paused momentarily, then resumed picking, but the eyes never wavered.

"You're in the Ministry, you can do something," she was saying.

"I've been posted overseas, that's why I'm asking you."

"Oh, I forgot. When are you going?"

"Few weeks' time."

He continued eating without speaking any further, his head bent, his face fixed on the food in front of him. There was a second man of dark brown complexion, jug-eared and with eyes like black pin-points. He knew they were looking at him between the bobbing heads and the weaving bodies of the other customers in the shop who conversed as they ate.

"I don't understand this at all," she said. "He loves to talk but he would never cause any trouble to anyone."

"How long since you last saw him?"

"Maybe seven eight years."

"That's why you don't understand. He's changed. You know he had a breakdown in university? He was in hospital for a spell."

"Why? For how long?"

"Not long. Things were all right after he got married. For a while. When he came back from England after studying law, he wouldn't settle down. The big firms were after him; one even offered him an immediate partnership. It seems he gave that firm an obscene reply. He's got his own firm now. You should see it. A real hole. He wants to help the masses, I suppose."

He caught sight of the two men again and he stiffened. A long silence ensued which made her feel awkward.

She pushed her chair back and said, "Well, I have to go." She shared the cost of the meal with him. As they walked out, one of the men loudly slurped his spittle through the side of his mouth. He tried hard to think that the sound was not directed at them. Outside on the grass verge they walked one behind the other, threading their way among the pedestrians, the din of the noon-day traffic precluding any conversation. At the next junction she turned briefly, and said, "They were making those sounds at us, weren't they?" Then she waved a hand, and disappeared into the crowd of people who crossed the road when the lights turned green.

· · ·

Tengku Sabariah said to him some days later that Panglima had called him on the telephone but she had put him off. "Why didn't you tell me?" he demanded.

"You so moody how to tell?" She searched his face. He walked into his room and picked up the receiver.

There was a *kampung* up north to which the trouble had spread, Panglima said. He needed someone to make an on-the-spot report quickly. Would Yun Ming do this last thing before he left the Ministry?

Yun Ming had a potential buyer coming to his apartment to look at his car; he had not even packed yet. Panglima was insistent. He had always counted on Yun Ming even in preference to his Malay officers to undertake inconvenient tasks.

Yun Ming asked, "What kind of trouble?"

"Nothing too serious," Panglima said, trying to make light

of it. "Some fellows broke something or other. Supposed to be holy. You know these young people nowadays. They don't really mean to harm. Simply fooling around. But they made some other people angry. Now it's a good thing that groups are on edge with each other. That way when we send a directive, everyone has to obey. But we must see to it that our own groups do not suffer. Just go and have a talk with people there. Find out what's really going on."

Panglima was the first highly-placed officer who really took Yun Ming as a friend after May 1969. They had met at a *muhibah* dinner, and began talking in earnest after they discovered that a relative of Panglima's owned property a few streets away from Yun Ming's father's house in Tranquerah in Malacca. Even if they hadn't spoken at length then, Panglima would have stood out; the high forehead, the square face and greying bushy hair at the back of his head; the narrowly slanted eyes that, behind thick-lensed horn-rimmed spectacles, seemed to glower. At this dinner, he did not pretend; he did not go around laughing heartily and slapping the backs of the Chinese and Indians present. But he caught in the intonation of Yun Ming's eagerly enunciated Malay a remorse beyond the personal for the events of thirteenth May. He stocked it carefully, referring to the people out of touch with the *rakyat* who were responsible for everything bad that had happened. Despite their education they were insensitive, they had no real social understanding. Yun Ming nodded his head several times.

On later occasions, they spoke of the obstacles to nation-building; so many different customs, so many religions. Yun Ming did not know for certain whether Panglima was speaking in praise or deprecation of this. The eyebrows were raised as he glowered at Yun Ming expecting him to show full comprehension of what he, Panglima, had said. Yun Ming found himself saying with fervour that the Chinese and the Indians had to forget where they came from. They must follow one way of life, have one way of doing things. He caught himself in time before being swept into saying they should have one religion. Panglima's pursed, lipless mouth widened slightly in approval. After an interval it was Panglima who, learning of Yun Ming's position in the Foreign Ministry, had asked that he be seconded to the Home Ministry for urgent work covering unity. Now Yun Ming was being moved again. He didn't mind. Everything was for the country and the nation.

"Oh and by the way," Panglima was saying, "Wan Nurudin is having a farewell dinner for you next Saturday after you come back. Ask anyone you like. Your wife here?"

"She's gone to England. With the boy."

"Will she join you in Bangkok?"

Yun Ming hesitated. "We haven't made any plans yet."

After trying for a few minutes not to call Sara, he eventually did. He said he would like to meet her again before he left and suggested lunch. He would give her the whole background of what Dahlan was up against.

She said, "I'm not free."

"How about Thursday?"

"Term time is not good. I have classes most days."

"Okay, then, Friday."

After some hesitation she agreed.

That was on Wednesday. On Thursday afternoon he got a call from her. She was sorry she could not make it. He had feared something like that would happen.

"How about another day?"

"I can't. I'm sorry."

He said, "Okay. Then come to my farewell party. It's at the Sec-Gen's place. Next Saturday." He gave her the address. "At least you can make sure I'll be going off."

She laughed and said she wasn't sure but she would try to be there.

3

Sara's father was not pleased to see her when she returned home to Sayong in Perak. "How can you come back when the holidays haven't even started?" Lebai Hanafiah grumbled.

"It's all right. I have not missed giving any classes. I've done all my work. I just wanted to be here. That's all."

"What about—" he stopped short, feeling that even he as her father should not intrude.

I know, Omar, she thought. That's what it was about.

Sayong was a little *kampung* along the Perak River which had changed only a little since the day when Sultan Iskandar Shah had stopped over during a pleasure trip upriver. A modest tarmac road about half a mile inland running parallel to the river bank confirmed that development had touched the *kampung* too. The road curved through fruit orchards for some miles before joining the main trunk road to Kuala Kangsar. There was other evidence of Government efforts to help it. A *balai raya* with faded notices about tuition times for little children stood on one of the lanes just off the main road. Next to it was a little wooden building which served as a small library and reading room. A couple of broken chairs and a table had been pushed to one side, the floor had not been swept for many days. Further along the main road was a modest-sized rice-milling factory which was not functioning. Beside it lay a tractor, many of its parts ripped of. Further inland two or three lanes threaded past the cluster of houses interspersed by rambutan and banana trees. The houses stood on high ground which sloped rapidly away on the further side through secondary forest to the bank of a tributary of the Perak River. Here the water meandered sluggishly in leafy shade, no longer overflowing its bank since the Government built a hydroelectric dam further upriver.

Sara loved the seclusion of her father's house away from the main road. Most of her childhood friends had grown up, married, and gone away. A few remained. She recognised Safiah among the crowd of neighbours now trooping into their house to watch television. When she was in Standard Four, Safiah's mother had died and her father took her out of school to look after her younger brother and two sisters. Safiah greeted her warmly, but their conversation, after the first exchange of news, was perfunctory. She had married young but marriage brought little change to her hard life. She now cultivated six *relongs* of *sawah* belonging to her husband, besides raising the five children she had before she was twenty-four. The light from the television screen made her face shine gauntly.

Outside there was the honk of a bread-seller's motorcycle horn and the tinkling bell of an ice-cream man. Sara and her father sat in the verandah surveying the evening scene, watching the dusk gathering into dark.

"Does he mind your coming back here this time?" he asked. "Did you ask his permission?" When she remained silent, he added, "Maybe young people nowadays don't discuss such things with each other. You just go when you want to. He just goes when he wants to."

She said, "He isn't at home. I don't know where he has gone."

Omar, her husband, would not be back for one week, he had said. He was in a group that had gone to Jerangau to look at the pioneering settlement started there by Tok Guru Bahaudin.

The next day Lebai Hanafiah conducted his religious class as usual. The sitting room of the house echoed with the children's chanting in unison. The girls' eager faces, framed by their white capes, shone in the morning sunlight which angled in through the open doors and carved wooden railings on one side of the house. Lebai Hanafiah sat crossed-legged, immobile, facing his charges, his sallow face expressionless, listening to the children's voices.

She walked into the compound, pausing to look at the red hibiscus flowers which hung on dropped stems as if in a cascade over the fence of a neighbouring house. The shadows of the coconut fronds made a zebra-like pattern on the sandy ground. The hibiscus exploded in her field of vision. She looked at the leaves and discovered a cavernous intricacy of delicate lights and shadows. One flower glowed so intensely bright that it seemed aflame and she gazed at it thunderstruck. She stood before a molten furnace-door. It gave as she reached to touch it, and she was confronted by a gulf of unfathomable gentian into which she floated deliriously. It was inexpressibly wonderful to the point of being terrifying and she steered away from the disquieting splendour, fearing madness.

She walked down to the river bank and sat in the shade of the angsana tree she had known since childhood. The river had eroded the bank so that now a large root of the tree lay exposed and seemed to wind its way into the soft shallows like a dark serpent. The shouts of the children splashing about in the river reminded her of days in the past when, after religious class, she and her friends raced down to bathe in the cool, flowing water.

In the afternoon she dandled Safiah's youngest child as Safiah herself winnowed the *padi*. Two older children, both boys, were spinning *gasing* with their friends on a sandy patch some distance away. Tall *pinang* trees lined the little two-acre patch which was their homestead, making it seem a cool haven in the expanse of dry stubble that stretched away all round where once the green *padi* plants had thrived. Karim, Safiah's husband, had gone to Kuala Kangsar.

Sara listened to Safiah's account of the season just ended. The tractor hired from the National Padi Board broke down several times. Then the rains did not come on time. But the *penyakit merah* was the worst. "We couldn't do anything," Safiah said. "All our work was no use. So many months we spent in the field, what has it brought us? Once those worms got into the grain we lost heart. The grain which we got breaks easily in the milling. Look," she stopped her desultory winnowing and taking a few grains of the *padi* between her fingers pressed hard and then showed the broken grain to Sara. "See? Half of our harvest will be like that. Lucky thing the government is going to help us, otherwise sure we cannot carry on. Already some of the families in our *kampung* don't want to plant anymore. Have you seen *sawah*? Not dug up anymore, nothing growing, just *lallang*. They just rely on the fruit trees. Nothing to do but pluck the fruit. Anyway," she lowered her voice, "There's trouble here now, you know. Work in the fields also not safe." When she asked Sara how things were in the city, her wistful tone of voice made Sara feel slightly guilty about her own comfortable life.

Later she picked up a bicycle and in jeans pedalled swiftly on the narrow metalled path that ran along the river bank for half a mile before turning inland. Her hair flew, she rang her bicycle bell in exhilaration, swerving past other cyclists and a few pedestrians. She passed a little *kedai* where several young men were seated on a makeshift bench outside. Some of them were barebodied. They shouted out to her teasingly, but she looked straight ahead as she rode on.

Some yards ahead a youth signalled to her to stop. He was dressed in city clothes, dark trousers and a clean shirt with sleeves folded up above the elbows. It seemed he wanted to say something to her. She stopped, standing astride her bicycle.

"I know you," he said, somewhat brusquely. "You were at the university club in Kuala Lumpur, no?"

She said nothing, wondering at his manner.

He had a thin moustache which made his brown-complexioned face look darker. He kept looking away and staring into the distance, as if to perceive something. When he looked at her, she saw that his eyes were red, as if with anger. "I speak to you like your brother. Dress properly, don't bring shame on your father and mother."

She remounted her bicycle and rode on without a word.

The Government advisory station for farmers was a simple hut with a green and white coat of paint, standing in a small fenced-in area. A signboard gave the times when the station would be open. It was shut when Sara got there. She got off her bicycle and stood staring at the hut from the gate. Suddenly it opened and a Chinese stood in the doorway. It was Yun Ming.

"What are you doing here?" she gasped.

He was smiling. "Shouldn't you be in the university?"

"This is my *kampung*."

"I know."

They laughed. It seemed as if the tinkling of the *gamelan* was wafted again in the rural air.

She said, "I came to see my father."

"Is he not well?"

"No, it's not that. He's all right,"

She took in the hut and the unswept garden in a glance.

"Is this place ever open?"

"When was the last time you saw it?" He walked up to the gate and opened it to let her in. "There is some trouble."

"I haven't come this side a long time." She walked with a nonchalance she did not feel. "What sort of trouble?"

He showed her in, switching on the solitary electric bulb which hung from the ceiling without a shade. It cast a yellow light over the sparsely equipped room. On an old wooden table lay a few files, a typewriter and a table fan. He switched the fan on. A faded poster about kinds of *padi* hung on the notice board, one of its corners curling. He sat on the table and talked about an old Hindu shrine which had been discovered is an archaeological dig some years ago. Its statues had been smashed, the shrine desecrated. The persons responsible were never caught. Two days after that a gang of youths came in two cars from the town, shouting abuse, making obscene gestures at passers-by in the village. It seemed they held the village responsible for what had happened. Sure enough there were a couple of brawls, and one person was stabbed and taken to the clinic where he spent an uncomfortable night before being sent to the hospital in Taiping. Soldiers now patrolled the main roads. He said, "I came up to see what needs to be done. Last job before I go."

"Are you thinking Dahlan might come here too?" She could not keep irony entirely out of her voice. "By the way, what is happening to him?" she asked.

"Depends on him."

She did not understand why he was so dismissive, simply because he happened to be going away. Come to think of it, she did not understand Yun Ming's role at all. She said, "Do you mean if he comes up here and speaks to people saying, don't desecrate this shrine, you'll put him in?" but the look on his face made her feel as if she had said something frivolous.

"He may come here. We think he is also planning to go to Jerangau. That would be dangerous."

She said, "We will probably be going there."

"To live there?"

"Yes. My husband wants us to live in Tok Guru Bahaudin's community." He felt repulsed and couldn't react immediately. He put his hands on the desk behind him and half sat on it. She had said the words with a certain deliberateness.

He said with odd formality, "He's a good speaker. Bahaudin, I mean."

"Is it true what they say of him?"

"I heard him give a *ceramah* when he came to KL last year— part of my duties," he added with a smile. "You know, you can't take your eyes off him when you're listening to him. It's like you're in a trance. People become spellbound when he speaks. Have you seen them? Their eyes become glazed, they sway from side to side."

She said, "Many people's hopes and aspirations are centred on him."

She saw he was going to challenge her, and she walked

away from him, inspecting the room, and reading the outdated circulars pinned on the notice board. "Here's one about *penyakit merah*." She went up close to the board and began reading it.

He stood beside her and glanced at it. "Yes. Advice on how to prevent it from taking hold. Not followed, you see."

Last year there were a few rice fields overgrown with weeds and *lallang*. This year there were going to be many more. There is a little insect that gets into the *padi* stalk, and when that happens there is little that can be done to get them out. This year people simply gave up. Many were just relying on their fruit trees. Mangosteens, bananas, rambutans, durians. One season after another. They got less, but they were certain of what they got. Why till the fields when more than half the crop could end up useless. When the fruits were in season they plucked them and sold them at stalls just round the corner from Iskandar Bridge. When that was over it was too late to till the fields, the season was gone, they had missed the cycle, but it did not matter. They had *rezeki*.

She caught an underlying appeal in his voice unrelated to the words he was uttering. She turned to look at him and realised he had never taken his eyes off her as he spoke, and she saw in his look no reticence. The words about the problems of the station continued to tumble out of his mouth, more haltingly. Now there was discontent in the *kampung*, and two factions which differed fiercely with each other as to how their problems should be solved, were beginning to have separate weddings and even separate funerals. Think of Dahlan coming into such a situation, and where were we?

She no longer was able to follow his words, the air in the room stifled her, sweeping her into disquiet. Trembling she reached out with her hand, but before he could take it she withdrew it and forced herself to look again at the curling poster. "Are you going to close this station down?" she heard herself ask.

It was some time before he spoke again. "We had an officer here. He organised courses. But the people stopped coming. After that he just collected his pay every month. We replaced him, but it was the same." He broke off. "Why are you here? Don't you have teaching to do? When are you going back? Do you have to leave the university to go to Jerangau?"

"The campus was dull," She said. "I came back after my studies, full of ideas I was going to thrash out with the students. No use. You feel you're being watched, your ideas are all carefully recorded and reported somewhere. You look over your shoulder when you say something. The students simply want to pass. The staff write rubbish in the local newspapers just so that they can say they have published something. There's a beautiful campus, shelves of books but it is a dead place. Everyone should go to Jerangau—or places like it." She was leafing through a large record book which was the office journal as she spoke. When she stopped and placed her hand on a page to make as if to read, he took it gently in his.

The sound of the fan receded, the sounds of the children's shouts outside were stilled. His hands grasped her body everywhere, hurting. He bit her lips till she cried with pain. She leaned against him as if forcibly propelled, and felt the ardour of his passion with an acquiescence which surprised her. She was moving in a subterranean channel whose current, swift and noiseless, sped her to a bank where all was still.

Sudden voices outside startled them and she wrenched herself away, panting.

She said, "Someone's coming."

He went unsteadily to the front of the office and stood listening for a while.

She whispered, "Who is it?"

"It's nothing. Just passers-by."

With shaking hands she tucked her shirt back into her jeans, and rearranged her hair. She did not look at him.

"Don't go. Please don't go."

She opened the door and walked slowly out without another word. She pushed her bicycle on the path leading up to the road, the gravel under the tread of her feet sounding unnaturally loud. From the corner of her eyes she saw again the dark, red-eyed youth who had accosted her earlier. He was sitting among companions on the wooden steps of a *kampung* house. She was aware only of his eyes fixed on her as she climbed on her bicycle. Someone sucked in his breath exaggeratedly, another gave a short laugh. She stood hard on the pedals to gather speed and rode away.

• • •

Her father said to her when she returned, "Where have you been? Why are you back so late? You know it's dangerous to go about alone."

Most of the television watchers had left the house. Light from the electric bulb which swung over the dining room crept uncertainly into the darkened living room yellowing the faces of those who remained. A mother, her sleeping child on her lap, sat on the wooden floor, continuing to gaze at the screen that flickered brightly with phantom shapes from another hemisphere. Two boys, sprawling on the floor jostled with each other to get a better view of the fleeting figures. The noises of the night had now become a soft, high-pitched whirr pressing upon the dimly-lit house in waves.

Panglima had come to visit.

People began to call him Panglima because, after the British reoccupation, he spoke often of the revival of religious values and of the cultural decay which the West had spread to the countries of South East Asia. He became a frequent visitor to the house of Lebai Hanafiah offering him advice on all matters, including Sara's education. If Lebai Hanafiah had any reservations, he kept them to himself. After all, Panglima was now Political Secretary to the Minister of Home Affairs but, more than that, the people of the *kampungs* surrounding Kuala Kangsar feared him for the secret knowledge he had acquired of themselves from the individual files compiled by the Ministry. Sara was only six at the time, and he noticed the more than common interest which Panglima showed in her.

As Sara grew to young womanhood, Panglima developed a passion for her he found more and more difficult to hide. Lebai Hanafiah instinctively knew he was going to be asked for her hand, and to avoid having to refuse him, hurriedly arranged for her to go to America "for further studies". The news of her marriage to Omar did not diminish Panglima's desire for her. He found the way she mixed easily with people of other races a convenient pretext to call on her frequently. It was sure to lead to trouble, he told her father, especially while Omar was away overseas. As an elder of the community he could not be refused, but Lebai Hanafiah was uneasy.

Sara listened to his low monotone in amazement as if hearing it for the first time. It was like the root of the tree by the river bank, snaking its way into the clear water. The words conveyed objectivity, the monotone a bitter venom. "Dahlan means well. But he is just a Western liberal. He is thinking this country is like the steps of Senate House in the University of London. He wants to be a martyr and, you know what? I guarantee he will be one if he does not look out, you see if I am wrong. He thinks he can just stand up and shout to make everybody listen to him. Then he will go into a pub, drink beer and read human rights poetry. After that he will go to bed with some white girl from a human rights group, and his conscience will be at peace, and he won't have to worry anymore about actually doing something about inequality, poverty, and race." Panglima spoke of the need to wipe out all traces of the colonial legacy and reassert the traditional heritage. "He used to be a real—banana! You know—brown outside, white inside. Now I do not say that, Macaulay said that." The teeth were bared in a genial smile at his own joke. "But he realised it. That he had to change. Look at him now. He works very hard. I can trust him just like our own people. I gave him a job to do here. He should be around." He broke off, and the eyes narrowed again into their habitual suspicious stare. "Have you seen him?" Sara, whose thoughts had wafted into the night, though she kept her eyes in a fixed stare on Panglima, did not hear him. "I said, have you seen him?"

What would this ape think if she lied? What, if she told the truth? The narrowed eyes, slanted at her from an inclined head, would even see deceit where none was. Her heart thumping, she said, "You mean, Yun Ming? Yes, I saw him at the station. What is he doing here?"

Panglima took a deep breath, and looked at the television screen for a while. "Did you know he was coming up to Sayong?"

"No, I did not."

He did not pursue the point. There was time. He said, more mildly, "He is doing work here which you could do better since this is our *kampung*. But you are looking for the spiritual life. If you weren't going to Jerangau, we could use your help.

We need people like you to explain things to the village folk." He paused, and his lidless eyes narrowed still more. "I could show you what to do."

Real social involvement, she thought. Providing people with the mental equipment to fight the decadence that was swamping the towns. But she recoiled at the thought of working with Panglima.

"Dahlan is a decadent," he was saying. We must stop his influence at all costs. Look at his name. Harry Dahlan. He likes their way of thinking so much that he does not know how much he has lost. They have put their mark on him."

On you. On me. On all of us. The thought filled her with an inner desperation. She had to find a way of reasserting what was native and true. The past clung to her, a large scab that had to be shed so that normal growth would be hers again even though a scar might remain.

Bright moonlight shone down on the *kampung*. From the verandah she saw dancing streaks of silver on the waters of the river. The chug of the ferry boat carrying its last passengers came faintly across in the night. It seemed as if the wake of the boat was moving towards her in a gentle, prolonged heave. It soothed her beating heart.

4

WHEN SARA CAME back from Sayong she found a note from Gita, the servant gone, and Omar back from Jerangau. He was sleeping late. She made some coffee for herself and ate a slice of bread and butter. Then she telephoned Gita. Gita said, "Where have you been? *Balik kampung*, ah? In the middle of term! Must be something important or—is anything wrong?"

"I'm okay, lah. Just had to see my father."

"Why? What is the matter?"

"It's nothing. He's okay."

"Why you didn't tell me you were going off? The next day only I knew. Your students were waiting outside your door. You had a tutorial. You forgot ah?"

"Yes. No."

"That fellow, your student, what's his name, Wah Loong, that's right. Just give me trouble only. Wants to know are you sick, wants to know where is your house—all sorts. I said, nothing doing, don't go bothering your lecturer, do your work only, enough. He never listen. Always pestering me."

"He's one of my good students. I wish," she murmured, but then did not know how to go on. After all she had deserted her class. What would Gita say if she told her that she had been on the edge of a strange shore.

Gita was busy with her own prattle. "…yeah, well, don't worry. I took some students, Roslan took some. But Fong— he was looking for you. That guy—only wants to make trouble. I simply bluffed him you were sick. Then I phoned your house. Phoned and phoned, no answer. So I put a message in your box."

"Thanks."

"Are you coming to the campus today? You better come, you know. Got nothing also never mind. Just show your face."

"I'm coming in the afternoon. I have a class."

She put down the receiver and stood motionless for a long time. She and Gita had been to school together. After Sixth Form, Gita went to a university in Kuala Lumpur, Sara got a scholarship to go to the States. When they met again they were lecturers in the same department, and in private slipped back to the old Malaysian English lingo. Gita's ailing father had made sure she did not marry. There was a story that he even came to the university once to stop a young man seeing her. After her mother's death Gita left her father in Petaling Jaya and, according to friends, lived it up. But her flippancy only partially hid the bitterness of her lost years. She enjoyed spurning the offers of Indian men who, she said, only wanted a domestic slave.

Omar had awakened and was in the kitchen. He said, "I saw Tok Guru Bahaudin again. He has told his people we're coming. So you can give your notice. We'll leave at the end of this month."

She said, "We should think about this carefully."

"No need. I've decided."

"After all, it's a major step." She tried to give her voice the objective tone she employed in tutorials. Inwardly she felt a panic.

He spoke about modern life and how it had become corrupt. Everywhere people were chasing money, living immoral lives. This was a godless time and he was lucky to find Tok Guru Bahaudin to help redeem his life.

"You should see how they live," he said, looking at her but his eyes were glazed. "The men do certain tasks, the women others. All the children are taught together according to their age groups. During the day there's weaving and planting and washing and working. And in the evening after prayers and the evening meal the leader gives everyone advice on daily problems. You know, people nowadays have forgotten what beauty there is in such simple life. I tell you, Sara, until you have seen it, you don't know."

"I know."

"How can you? Only if you hear him, you will know what I mean."

He was eager. At the same time he was trying to make it sound as if she would be deviating if she did not agree. Tina Turner was singing "What's love got to do with it?" on the neighbour's television. Her raunchy tones wafted disdainfully into their room.

She got up and filled a glass of water.

"You know Sanusi?" he said. "Never prays, drinks a lot with those yellows at the club, great ladies' man. You see him now you'll never recognise him. He attended one of the meetings. Just one, and that was enough."

She tried to listen. "I think we are all religious deep down but we have forgotten it. After Sanusi heard Tok Guru Bahaudin he resigned his job. He took his daughters from the convent. He distributed pamphlets, started going to mosque twice a day. Last month he moved with his entire family to Jerangau."

She was troubled that he seemed moved by genuine religious zeal whereas she felt nothing. Resolutely she addressed her mind to thinking something constructive but she found the effort boring. She had seen others with the same sweaty unwashed look which Omar showed this morning—as if that was the badge of revelation. Some of them had joined communities designed to pursue the ideal life strictly. They took their children out of schools, they collected together their meagre savings, they sold their belongings and went into the wilderness to build a good life away from the pollutions of modern living. And what was wrong with that? Why, nothing. That too was a way of reasserting what was native and true.

But if she followed that way she would have to shut her mind to everything and imagine it had never happened. She would have to regard everyone who didn't think like her as not worth talking to: where would Gita be, Wah Loong, her students. And Yun Ming.

He said, "You have got it all wrong, you know. You think we have no learning?" Her Western education had blinded her, he said. She didn't know her own heritage but went and learned the white man's. She had taken a path that deviated from true knowledge. She actually belittled the learning and spiritual accomplishment of her own tradition. What was needed was disciplined living to realise it once again. Here we have all the immoral publications, television and imitation lifestyles, but no thinking, no reflection. Rather then be swallowed up by these, better to go and find a quiet place to restore oneself to serenity and peace.

Sara too had often thought like this. His words created uneasy stirrings of feelings that formerly derived their vitality from exposure to the whole spectrum. She should try to let the spectrum be narrowed. He spoke with forceful emotion, speaking to her, it seemed, out of love, not anger. Her friends were all right, but take Gita, she was a distraction and ultimately a danger. The same could be said of the others. No need to cut them off completely, but if they wanted to live with little or no religion and pray to idols, they should be kept at a distance. It troubled her that he was not sad when he said this.

The look on her face made him stop for a moment, but he spoke even more earnestly. "I know what you're thinking, you don't believe me. I know my life before did not have much meaning. I drank. I didn't say my prayers. I even ate *haram* things. And—and—I know I haven't made you happy. That is why, don't you see?"

He tried to touch her hand but she drew it away.

She pushed her chair back and stood up. She said, "I have a class."

"Can't you stay and talk a little?" He was actually pleading, she marvelled.

"It's late. Someone will report me."

He was stung by her lack of interest. "Where did you go yesterday?"

"I went to see my father."

"Are you going with another man? Where were you last night?"

"I told you. Now I have to get dressed. I have missed some classes. I have to make them up, I have a lot of reading to do. You see I haven't written up my lectures yet."

She went upstairs, took a shower and put on a *sarong kebaya*. In his new frame of mind he might disapprove of the outfit but she didn't care. Just because he talked about morality the way he did why should it be taken for granted that he was more religious than she?

He was in the sitting room reading a newspaper. As she walked past him to the door she knew that he had been only lying in wait.

He said, "When are you coming back?"

"I'm not sure. Evening, some time."

"If you come back early—"

"Can't promise."

"Sara, we have to discuss."

She was now irritated. She said shortly, "No point, *abang*, what is there to discuss? You have never discussed anything with me. You have decided everything."

He flung his paper down and came up to her. "Why are you behaving like this? I am speaking to you nicely, why can't you speak nicely?"

His agitation startled her. His fists were clenched and he was trembling. His curly hair was dank and glistening, his face shiny and serious. His hands were stuck in the pockets of his black Malay *baju* open at the neck with a copper stud in the collar. That was how he had looked that evening in New York when his father who was an attachè gave a party for Malaysian students within three hours' driving distance. Sara who was at Temple University took the bus ride to New York, eager to meet other Malaysians and catch up on home news. Amidst the chatter that evening in Encik Abdullah's luxury flat, stepping round and over students sprawled on cushions on the floor, Omar had come up to her. He wore a medallion draped round his neck, and a serious look which seemed to hide a smile. They had danced and his touch seemed like fire. That was eighteen months ago.

She now saw that their relationship had never progressed

beyond that first evening. To pretend it was anything else was plain dishonesty. In the States they lived a charade: they went to football games like American teenagers, they held hands and ate hamburgers and watched the mini-skirted pom-pom girls whirling their coloured streamers in circles and semicircles, and kicking their legs high. She felt excited and told herself how happy she was. Omar looked very American in his jeans, college tee-shirt and baseball cap: his speech took on an additional nasal twang to match the tone of the Americans he spoke to.

Once he suggested that they might go to a motel: she pretended not to hear him; when he pressed her she said, "No" shortly, and he was silent for a long time. Some weeks later he asked her to marry him and the memory of their first evening in New York revived in her. She clung to it, accepted his proposal and wrote to her father, spurred by the promise of even better things to come.

A few months after their marriage, he had gone away for six weeks on a tour with some Iranian and Pakistani students. When he returned he had become withdrawn, and spoke to her less. It was as if a blight had fallen.

He spoke as if there could be no other view but his. The frivolity that had been an engaging part of his character had disappeared. Instead the chin was drawn in tightly, the eyes glistened and when he spoke the words fell from his lips with a calm satisfaction that brooked no dissent and left her uneasy. She did not know how to regard him.

Back in Malaysia, here in the university flat with standard cane furniture, and a balcony overlooking a road that became congested with hawkers' stalls every evening, where in recent months Omar's friends came to talk in low tones of the spell-binding *ceramahs* being given in Jerangau, the foreign accretions to his style of behaviour evaporated, he cultivated a stubble beard and he slipped more easily into the habit of waiting for her to attend to his wishes.

She became aware that he did not talk with her as an equal; and he showed irritation when she tried to join in any discussion with their friends. One day as she placed a tray of glasses of syrup for them on the low table round which they sat and he continued talking without a flicker of recognition of her presence, she felt a vile sense of inferiority. She saw his lower lip hang out with the relish he felt over a comment he was making: it looked detached from his chin, and she turned away repelled. She fell into a routine where, except for sex, they lived separate lives. She was glad to have the house to herself whenever he went outstation for his prayer meetings. After one spell when he made several trips in the space of three months and was hardly home, he didn't touch her. She blamed herself, then him, and finally threw herself into her university teaching, trying to avoid the thought that pressed on her mind insistently and gave her no peace.

"The students are waiting for me," she said, more mildly.

"I want to talk to you about our plans. There's so much to do before we go to Jerangau. I know you're worried about leaving everything and going there. But don't worry, when you hear Tok Guru Bahaudin you will know, he's so clear, so rational, so moving, he doesn't try to trick you. When he speaks it's so simple, so wonderful, so natural." He had recovered his breath now and spoke carefully. "Let's talk about our future life in Jerangau."

Her lectures on Levi-Strauss were a flop, she thought. It was small comfort that the students scribbled away furiously as she spoke. She felt an imposter. At the end of one morning she returned to her room and hastily packed her books. The telephone rang. The operator told her someone had called twice. Would she like to speak to him? The number was—

"Yes," she said. While waiting for the call to come through she marked a few students' essays and then decided to cancel the call. The telephone rang. It was Yun Ming.

He said, "Hullo, did you get back all right?"

"Yes."

After a silence he said, "You said you were maybe going to leave the university and go to Jerangau. Are you really going?"

She laughed self-consciously and broke into dialect. "No, lah, not yet decide one." Then she said, "Yes, we are going." An exact date had not been decided, but she would leave the university at the end of the month.

"Before you go, will you call me?"

"You will be gone by then. How to tell?"

"Can I call you? Can we meet again? Just once."

"Is it all about Dahlan again?"

There was a teasing effervescence in her voice. He was unlike any man she had ever known. He seemed to have no politics, yet by the way he spoke, he reminded her again of a wider world that she had dreamed of. She had accepted that it had been smashed, but here he was, a blithe reminder that it was there all the time.

When she saw him in the last evening of the seminar he was obsequious to all. Yet there was a curious reserve even when he spoke to someone like Wan Nurudin, for example. A half-smile played on his features; and whether sitting or standing, there was a stillness of posture which his listener mistook for attentiveness. Over the telephone speaking to her, his voice sounded level, with just a tremor in it. She could not believe he was going to be posted overseas soon.

She told him it was true she was feeling increasing dismay at the persistent unrest in different parts of the country. There was no leadership by example. Every group was fighting tooth and nail for itself. The hope for unity based on equality had been forgotten. In the university she found it ridiculous to participate in a process of learning by decree and by handouts. She was vexed with herself for being impatient, for not trying to understand the total situation and then she was vexed at pillorying herself for nothing. These things she said to him in simple words and halting sentences, amazed she was saying so much. Yun Ming asked again if they could meet. First she said yes; then she said she had a lot of things to do before leaving. She excused herself and put the receiver down suddenly.

That evening after she returned from the university she cooked a fish curry and some *sayur lodeh*. She took a shower and put on her favourite *baju kurung* then waited for Omar to return from wherever he had been to. When they sat down to eat, she served him and said, "*Abang*, I'm sorry about this morning."

He looked up, his face expressionless, and then continued eating.

At last he said, "The people are blind. This is not a real country."

"What do you mean?"

"Just look around you, what do you see? If we were all of the same faith, it would be a different matter." He swept the remaining curried rice from his plate with his fingers and deftly placed the food in his mouth. Leaning back he let his left arm hang loosely down the side of his chair. His upper lip beaded with a thin line of perspiration, he munched the last of his food with a soft squelching sound.

She said, "The problems cannot be solved in that way."

He looked at her for the first time during the meal, the lips widening in a smile. "That's what I'm saying. You don't know. You have not heard him. You will understand when we go there."

She placed the *kendi* before him and poured water over his fingers. As she collected the dishes and took them to the kitchen a few at a time, he continued, "We will leave on the last Friday morning early, we can get to Jerangau by five."

So she had a two-week breather.

She drove to the university early each morning and found it a relief to be in the middle of the traffic snarl instead of within the confines of their house. When there wasn't a curfew or a military checkpoint, it was diverting to observe the drivers from Petaling Jaya wedging their cars into every little gap that appeared amidst the gleaming banks of metal. Petrol fumes filled the air making her feel slightly nauseous. A Mitsubishi shot ahead of her from nowhere and switched on amber blinking lights to indicate it was going to cut into her path regardless of what she did. She normally blocked such intruders but today she let this one cut in. She drew her breath in sharply when she caught sight of the driver. It was not Yun Ming after all, although in the height and build and seen from a car behind, the resemblance was striking.

After she had given her tutorials, she sat in her oddly-shaped room listening to the rain as it poured continuously outside her window on the old rubber trees that had escaped felling when the Social Sciences 'A' Block had been constructed. On the other side of the chain-link fencing, the leaves and branches bobbed up and down under the pelting showers.

What a different scene this was to the snow-touched branches of the conifer pines that she could see from the window of her room in State College. She would put on her snug wind-cheater, cover her head with a woollen cap with its cone-top bent rakishly like a jester's. She would walk along the mall, stopping to sit on a bench and watch the students go by. Once a squirrel scrambled up to within a foot of her and pretended to grub around for food. She took a walnut and held it out coaxingly to him. It was fully five minutes before he came near and accepted it from her fingers. She was inwardly so excited she could not breathe. Passing students looked at her and walked on. The entire scene, the patches of snow, the strolling students, the little squirrel and his two shyer companions, the cold winter air, the stately College of Arts building at the far end of the mall filled her fleetingly with a sense of human beings in harmony with each other and with nature.

•   •   •

Gita said, "Harmony, my foot. I know you got married in the States, and I'm told some of the country campuses are beautiful, but—"

"I really felt it, Gita. I don't care what you say."

"Harmony of human beings—don't joke. Tell me, did you see many blacks about? Chicanos, American Indians? You don't have the answer."

"I know what you are trying to say. There wasn't any real harmony, it was just an illusion, I know, I know. But I've never felt like that there, illusion or no illusion."

Gita spoke emphatically. "Here you have to live. There you were on holiday, know what I mean? You didn't have to care two hoots about anybody. The worst that could happen to you was getting a fail grade in one of your courses." She broke off and said, "Ay, I'm sorry I interrupted you."

Gita had dropped in for a chat. She was brown, round-faced and good-looking. Today she was in shirt and slacks. When she wore a sari with a barer than usual midriff, her well-formed figure made her seem like a dancer come to life out of a classical Indian sculptured frieze. Gita's two brothers had married and gone away.

Sara spoke suddenly. "Do you know what it is to feel when you have made a mistake you can't correct?"

"What are you talking about?"

"I've been feeling like that for some time now."

Gita's voice had an edge when she said, "I had to live with a mistake for five years. I might have done so until the day I died." She got up and strode a few steps. "You know what?"

"You got out."

"Yup."

"I know. Gita, take care. Dahlan could be trouble. And what about your father?"

Gita said, "What about him? That's what I said to my married brothers when they tried to pass the buck to me. 'We've got our families to look after,' they said. I said, 'What about me, what about my life?' Still I suppose I would have looked after him. But after what he did to me, never!"

The rain had started again and was now becoming a heavy downpour. The first crack of lightning, more precise than a whiplash, shot down the wires and made them wince. The bolt of thunder, it seemed, exploded just above them. They watched in silence as more brilliant jagged lines lit the sky. Sara was waiting for the rolling thunder to die down but Gita was talking again, not caring whether she was heard or not. "Dahlan's okay. I'm happy to be with a human being who's back to basics. Yeah, he's an idealist. He'll get out of it. Anything is preferable after what I've been through. You remember the time my father came to the university and slapped me? In front of all my friends. Students also. Surely you remember? Ah no, you were in the States, right? Well, I'm sure you must have heard about it, our colleagues are such gossips."

Sara remained silent.

"You know what was my mistake? I should have told him to go to hell. I was going to marry Ravi and he broke it up, my father broke it up. For no reason. He said, I remember his words to this day, 'Of necessity there cannot be a marriage.'" Gita stopped and spat the words out, "Do you know what was the necessity? Ravi was a lower caste." After a few moments of brooding, she resumed, "I couldn't save it after that. Ravi broke off. And then—" Gita stopped and smiled. "No other young men came by. Men. What gives them the right to be gods over us? Why did my father have such power? You know why? Because I gave it to him, that's why. Well, I've taken it back."

Not long after she got back to her house, Omar told her that Gita was on the telephone. His colleague, Sabapathy, had dropped in with his wife for a visit, and as Sara took the receiver she could see how, in their tiny drawing room, Omar and their guests were poised to listen. She composed her face and said softly, "Hullo, Gita."

"Ay, you know when we were talking this morning?" Gita said. "How come I was doing most of the talking? Sorry to give you my life history uh."

"That's okay."

"You remember you said something about a mistake that cannot be corrected? You never told me, you know."

Sara spoke louder than usual. "Yeah, I can do your tutorial for you tomorrow. Don't mention it. Sure. That's okay."

"Hey, wait a minute, not so fast. What's this about a tutorial?" Gita said. "There's a message I have for you. From Wan Nurudin's secretary. Invitation to *makan malam* at his house. This Saturday. Farewell to someone or other. Wah, going with the big shots, eh?"

"No, lah, I think the invitation is for my husband. That's all."

"Are you going?"

Sara simply said, "Yes."

Sara was still trying to gather her wits together. She could not make out Omar. Sabapathy and he had been in Harvard together studying business administration. The two were laughing convivially as they recalled the lecturing peculiarities of some of their course professors.

"*Intan*, you should have seen Rinker," Omar said, greeting

her on her return from the university. They were caught in a fit of giggles.

"And heard him," Sabapathy added. He wore a moustache, Burt Reynolds style, and looked lean and fit.

The old jokes about Rinker she could put up with, but she could not stand the false endearment. *Intan*. She looked at his face. It was clear and smiling. She went into the kitchen saying she would get them something to drink.

When she brought in the tray with glasses of pink cordial, she could see Omar out of the corner of her eye beaming at her. He was proud that she was his wife. There she was, lighter-skinned than even many Chinese, the nose in profile straight but not unduly prominent like Indian noses, and a complexion that reddened slightly in the right places. He looked at her rounded hips as she bent slightly to serve a glass of rose syrup to Sabapathy and could not for a moment do his duty as a host to attend to what Mrs. Sabapathy, who was rather plain, was saying.

They had come to get his signature for a petition they were planning to send to the Government for funds to build an extension for their temple. It was all part of the spirit of good neighbourliness, Sabapathy said. Especially in these times it would be a good gesture for unity. He and his friends often supported Muslim and Christian causes, and see, *here* and *here*, oh and many other places, Muslims too had signed the petition. Sabapathy was rearranging the dogeared foolscap sheets on which signatures had been collected when his wife took up the appeal. The temple was an old structure of brickwork on a concrete foundation with plank walls and a zinc roof. It was on sloping ground and a major road ran alongside it. Recently the road was widened out to take heavier traffic but as a result the floor of the temple on one side cracked and was sinking and—

Sara, watching Omar, saw his eyes narrow as he looked at Sabapathy sideways. Occasionally he nodded his head slightly but otherwise he remained still.

When Sabapathy had finished, Omar looked thoughtful, coughed once or twice and then said, "Saba, now is not the time to do this, man, you know that. The trouble's got worse everywhere. Last night—you heard the latest?—some group has taken over several villages in the Northern Zone. Those fellows will come for me if they knew I helped you."

Sabapathy said, "You would be setting a good example. Especially as you are going soon to Jerangau, I hear."

Omar shook his head. "No, man. Very difficult nowadays, man, you know that. Any petition, no matter what kind also I think it's better for me not to get involved. Even for a good cause." He launched into an account of how he had supported several appeals for funds in the past and had been reprimanded by his superiors. "They're very strict now," he concluded.

All were silent for a while. Sara said, "Do you want my signature, Saba? I can sign."

"Thank you. Yes, yes, of course."

While Sabapathy quickly flipped the foolscap pages to the place where Sara was to sign, Omar from his comfortable armchair watched them, a half-smile slightly playing on his face, only the stillness of his figure betraying his disapproval.

After their guests had departed, Omar and Sara turned back to their living room in silence. He stood around aimlessly for a while, then sat down and picked up a newspaper. She collected the empty glasses, walked to the back and brought their food out to the table.

"You shouldn't have signed," he said as they ate. "You only encourage them."

"What? They're your friends."

He switched on the television and sat motionless in front of it. "Is he the man?"

She walked to the kitchen.

"Answer me. Is Saba the man you're going with? Do you want to make yourself filthy?" He was still motionless; she still said nothing.

She shut the doors and windows of their apartment and went into the bedroom. At the dressing table, she sat down. It was a sultry night and the fan did little to allay the sweat that covered her face and arms. The windows remained shut because Omar wanted them that way. She saw in her mirror the set expression on his face as he came in and she quailed.

"You are going with that fellow, right? That's why you are behaving like this. Answer me, are you?"

She said quietly, "How can you speak of your friend like that?"

"Why do you care? Is it because you have come together?"

He turned her shoulders round and slapped her hard.

"Stand up."

"Please, *abang*, don't do this."

"Stand up."

She stood up finally before him and he pushed her roughly on to the bed.

He took her that night, the first time in many months. She was startled, she said she was tired, but he was implacable. She eluded his grasp but he snatched at her wrist and held it until it hurt. She squirmed, turning her face aside to avoid his. She won free momentarily and moved away. She caught sight of the naked anger in his countenance.

"Who is the man you've got," he said in a fury. "You've got someone, haven't you?"

She shook her head, too frightened to speak. The next instant his fist landed on her ear, stunning her not so much by its force as by its unexpectedness. In a daze, she watched him come upon her, his eyes unseeing, his arms and legs flailing. He shook her limp body. Violently. She saw him struggle repeatedly. He stopped to rest briefly, then he struggled again. Finally he pushed hard at her, and lay breathing heavily. He did not say anything to her. She thought of Sayong and how the chug of the ferry coming in on the waves of the night had stilled her beating heart.

They did not speak to each other the next day. Something like an invisible force field had arisen between them. When they did speak on household matters, their words bounced off the unseen barrier in echoes.

5

IN THE EVENINGS Dahlan worked in the narrow cubicle that was his office with an intensity that he recognised was not doing him any good. He emerged from his work sessions as if waking from a long sleep, to find most of his staff gone except for his despatch clerk who was playing carom with his counterpart from the insurance firm next door. Outside his window, the sky loomed dark above and behind the haze thrown up by the lights of the city. He thought: I am fooling no one but myself. He had thought of himself as someone who 'cared'; he was surprised to find how little the thought actually governed his life. He let the demands of his clients absorb him each day. As he switched off the office lights and stepped out into the darkened corridor, locking the door behind him, placidity overtook him as he contemplated the long hours of attention he had given to resolving other men's concerns. The street lights cast a pallor on his face that made him look near death. In the mornings, he awakened with a slight sense of panic which, in vanishing with a new day's absorptions, left him thinking: I am fooling no one but myself.

He did not want to live with Anisah. His parents had arranged the marriage after he had completed his university studies. No matter that it was only a general degree, he was the small town boy who had made good. He said little when he was told the girl was the daughter of a neighbour who was one of the state assemblymen for Batu Pahat. They had played together as children. As a sex-starved undergraduate, he had had gonorrhoea once, and he thought so long as she had a reasonably pretty face and was not deformed, it was convenient not to have to go among the Imbi Road girls again. When he left his trainee executive officer's position in Sanderson's, the chemical company, to go to England, he sent her back to Batu Pahat with their son to stay with his parents. He came back after three years with a barrister's qualification and the knowledge that his marriage was futile.

His pursuit of the law was his other failure. He worked out of a little room which he rented in the UMBC building on Jalan Tun Perak. The old lift with space only for four creaked and groaned up to the top floor which had been divided into a warren of little offices. After he had moved in, he discovered that the roof leaked and the bucket which Susan, his accounts clerk, had ready, was not always enough to hold the water that dripped down. The work came in steadily and he was in his office most evenings till after seven. Alone under the fluorescent lighting of his room as the evening darkened and the roar of traffic in the street below seemed louder, the case of A. Neelambigai alias Fatimah binti Abdullah, 22, revealed his new profession to him as equally a futility. He did not stop attending to his clients; if anything his absorption in them became deeper. It was only when he was in his car driving home in the dark that the fate of Neelambigai, the young woman whose body neither her relatives nor the Religious Department would claim, exercised him.

Her mother would not speak directly to Dahlan when he went to the house to offer help. Using certain words she said, in effect to the empty air, "What for some people come and give trouble only." The old woman's eyes were streaked red with grief and anger, her matted grey hair hung in twisted strands.

Neelambigai's sister who stood behind weeping quietly, burst out, "She converted already, how can bury her. You want to bury—bury lah!"

Dahlan softly explained he came only as a friend, not as an official. He stepped out of their hut. A few wilted white jasmine flowers and withering palm leaves lay scattered on the ground outside. There was a blackened area of sand nearby: it could be where Neelambigai set herself on fire. Three Indian youths from the house opposite stared at him unremittingly. All around were similar-looking plank shacks with rusted zinc roofs made more dingy by an overcast sky. It had been raining steadily for a while: the path that snaked without plan between the shacks was muddy, and smartly dressed Indian, Chinese and Malay girls returning from offices stepped gingerly round patches of water. He passed a Chinese house with a high, whitewashed wall and an intricately designed gate for frontage.

It was like an assertion that the sprawling cluster of shanty dwellings surrounding it didn't exist. A middle-aged man in striped pyjamas and singlet who sat in an armchair just inside the gate said something loudly in Cantonese as he passed.

At the department they used other words, creating in the air a turbulence that made Dahlan feel faint. "Certainly we must bury her if we have the proof," said the Assistant. He wore a shiny white tunic shirt with gold studs and a white skull cap. He smiled benignly at Dahlan and leaned forward. "Are you her husband? If you are the husband, no problem, then we are assured." He waited but Dahlan was looking at the files on the shelves behind the official thinking that they too were full of words. The Assistant's word rang in his ears as he walked out. "These people they say—say only, how to know?"

He found it was not a simple case of him walking up to the mortuary and saying to those who denied her recognition, "I don't care for your beliefs, I will bury her." It was dark when he entered the General Hospital grounds, the end of visiting time, and relatives of patients streamed out of the entrance carrying umbrellas, plastic bags bulging with articles and food containers.

He ignored the nurse who tried to stop him at the main door and walked down a long corridor; turning numerous corners till he reached the mortuary at the back. A watchman stopped him and directed him to an office where, through a glass window, he saw a clerk eating fried noodles out of a packet. Dahlan waited until he had finished and then knocked on the door.

The clerk said, "Beginning to smell already. You mean to say you want to bury her? Are you from the department, *encik*, you're not from the department, how can? Not say I don't want to help. Just give me your authorisation letter, sure I will release it. Haven't got, means I got no choice. You're not a relation, are you a relation? Don't mind I ask, how come you want to meddle? I tell you, uh, *encik*, don't worry. Tomorrow the workers will bury her. No, I cannot give you the body, who are you, tell me that?"

He left the mortuary thinking he was no better than they. He too relied only on words for a living. He too used words to suit his object, not to approach the truth. That the truth was sometimes arrived at in his profession was incidental. It did not show that he cared. But Gita, to whom he confided his tentative plans, was not encouraging. What purpose could it serve speaking in front of the Malacca Cathedral, it would only get him into trouble. Even if the police did nothing, it was dangerous. There were many people, you never knew what they might do to you.

His late evenings of work began about then, also his headaches which returned for the first time since his university days. When he was unseeing after he got back to his house on the road to Kepong, Gita fed him and let him sit staring at the television for a while.

After their Sixth Form days, their paths had not crossed. In the university; they moved in different circles. He was in the Socialist Club, she was in athletics, a champion sprinter. When he was in England for his law studies, she became a lecturer in her university.

They met for the first time in years during rehearsals for the Bahasa Malaysia production of *Rashomon* in the old Town Hall. Dahlan felt as if he were seeing her for the first time. Gita's chiselled features without a trace of makeup, and her long hair glistened under the lights of the old dressing room. Her lashes drooping, she was conscious of Dahlan's gaze as she fitted the leading actress with her costume, and turned to look at him.

He laughed. "You're surely not that pig-tailed girl who was in the same class as me in school."

She said, "You were busy running after the other girls, how can you remember?"

"I wanted to know you better even then, but you were out of bounds."

She said, "How's that?"

"Remember your father used to pick you up after school? He was pretty fierce."

After rehearsal, they walked to the open air stalls in Campbell Road where they ordered *satay* and savoured the aroma of the grilling meat which wafted upwards in thin wisps of smoke from the hawker's glowing coals. She was thankful he did not embark on an artificial reminiscence of their school days. Instead they talked about the play. She could not make up her mind who in *Rashomon* was telling the truth, she said; the wife, the husband, or the brigand. Dahlan said he didn't know either. Everybody spoke a different language, everybody used different words, everyone was hurt and angry that the others did not understand them. The husband was a nobleman steeped in traditional ways; he expected everyone to speak in his accents. His wife coming from another province struggled hard to enunciate the sentiments he held dear, but many nights she lay awake, trying to still the turbulence in her breast caused by memories of her old life with her parents. When this— this—*thing*, this violence happened, she could no more stop the resurgence of her old way of speaking than she could stem a flood. The brigand, understanding neither, rejoiced in their mutual incomprehension. His words embodied an obscene truth that the others sought to shut their ears to. Everyone relied on the words of their own language.

Gita was staring wide-eyed at a group of men who had stood up suddenly at a table a few yards away and were advancing with expressionless faces, towards them, it seemed.

"We better go," she whispered.

He turned his head and she saw the fear in his bloodshot eyes as he got up with a jerk, pushed the flimsy structure of their table away, and walked with her to the exit. People at other tables looked at them, rose hurriedly and began to run.

Suddenly the hawkers on the roadside were packing their wares and pushing their barrows away. There were shouts in Malay and Cantonese. People ran in different directions. From the neon-lit coffeeshop came the sounds of crashing crockery and of its wooden shutters being put up. Gita and Dahlan ran towards the road, then turned back when they heard a voice shouting contemptuously, "*Melayu!*" On the road, traffic had come to a standstill, car horns blared. As they turned away, Dahlan saw a car surrounded and heard the sounds of splintering glass and the thud of rock on metal. A chorus of voices in different languages echoed against the old two-storey shophouses on Campbell Road and rose into the undiscriminating air.

Gita went back with him that night to his house which was several miles outside the city. From the pitch dark of the surrounding trees, the shrill sounds of the cicadas pressed upon their ears in waves. They groped their way up the steps of his house which stood on raised ground and was elevated on tall wooden supports. Unlatching the door, he sank to the smooth wooden floor, still in darkness, wordlessly pulling her down with him, and placed his mouth on hers roughly. She put her arms round him with ready fervour; he was grateful for the absence of coyness on her part. The night was no longer for them. They could see through the open door the dark silhouetted trees, and heard, far away, the occasional car go by. She saw the lines of his sombre visage clearly; he saw still after-images of the paraffin lamps of Campbell Road. They were like glowing fires on an empty landscape. He thought: I am fooling no one but myself. All my life I have been running away.

Gita asked, "Who were those men?"

He said, "I don't know."

She persisted. "Were they coming for you?"

"I don't know."

He was different now from earlier in the evening at the *Rashomon* rehearsal. Then there was a boyish eagerness in his manner. His hands waved the air as he argued with Nordin, who was directing, over the right interpretation of the play. He had, simply, a gift for words, enunciated with relish and immediately attracting attention. He had spoken with the same eloquence at public meetings. She found it a novelty to let herself be drawn to him.

He said that after the last forum he spoke at, he had received a few threatening letters. Nothing very dangerous, just expressing outrage at his views and demanding that he cease or he could be "in trouble".

His yellowing teeth set in determination, he said, "These people, who are they, they think they can stop me. Just let them wait and see. I'll show them."

She found his vehemence beguiling. She had not come across one so clearly bent on wasting the chances that had been thrown his way. In an age when the major revolutions were over, he was interested in making gestures, he wanted attention. She felt sorry for him and was curious to see how he was going to fare. She felt it was worth bucking against tradition for him. So she stayed with him often, and listened while he spoke critically on the Government's tardiness in acting against religious bigots and the advocates of forced cultural assimilation. Occasionally, when she interposed with a comment of her own, he looked surprised, and after a few moments resumed his critique. In the months that followed, his energetic speech took on a defiant ring. She spoke less when she saw he was not aware of the futility of his defiance.

But in the bar room in the old High Court building where the pursuit of truth was not the object, he was well regarded. Here where the talk over coffee, in between the hearings in judges' chambers, was about the housing estate patiently stalked and cunningly wrested from the speaker's grasp by a devious colleague, Dahlan speaking his mind on the plan to inject religious values into the administration was listened to, outwardly, as a novelty. No one joined him in discussion. He could take liberties regarding what he talked about which they could not. He, after all, was Malay. His forthrightness made them uneasy, and they showed by the ostentatious distance from which they listened to him across the large table that they did not necessarily endorse his opinions, even as many secretly did.

In the Selangor Club one evening, Gita had seen the wife of a lawyer grow silent as Dahlan talked, his eyes bulging, his unbuttoned cuffs flapping and then the young woman, fashionably dressed in a fitting *sarong* and blouse, with rouge on her cheeks and hair neatly coiffured for the evening out, blurted to her companion that Dahlan had no shame speaking of his race in this way. It was done quietly. The others in the party would not have noticed, but Gita, contrasting the woman's stony look with Dahlan's restless speech, which now began to appear hysterical, saw for the first time in Dahlan, behind the attractive preoccupied air, a childish petulance which was the more ludicrous for being found in a shabby, slightly balding, unkempt with bulging eyes. Dahlan did not stop talking; he did not seem to be aware of the impact he had created. But he did know and he was hurt. He returned sullen from their evening out, saying little: it was the beginning of his detachment, soon to become revulsion, from his life as a lawyer.

These lawyers, he told Gita, provided pseudo-learning in the marketplace for a price; it did not really matter to them who governed, their services would continue to be needed. She contradicted him mildly; not only the lawyers, there were others too. After brooding on that for a while, he told her curtly that she didn't understand. Sure there were others, but he wanted to get away from talking about factions. Well then, aren't the lawyers a faction, she asked.

He stared at her and then remained silent. He desperately wanted her to admire him for spurning the opportunities given to *bumiputras*, for making it on his own, and even more, for actually wishing to bait the conscience of the authorities on the religious issue. He had by his outspokenness already lost much; he would lose more including the regard of many decent compatriots of his; he might even lose his freedom. But what, after all, had he done? He had merely expressed his views to colleagues and friends with a similar educational background to his. After the evening at the Selangor Club, a sense of futility overtook him. Every morning he went to court and then to his law office where he worked till late, often interrupted by the thought: I am fooling no one but myself in thinking I can change anything.

That was when he undertook the defence of Ti Shuang, the leader of the spiritual movement who had been arrested by the police. Ti Shuang's real name was Ang Ju Piau. He was about forty years old with a round, florid face that was nonetheless good-looking. He was brought out of the lock-up still dressed in stained white tunic. His aides, a thin sallow-faced man of about thirty-five and a sturdy woman with a straight fringe dressed in a white blouse and black skirt, who had brought Dahlan to the Jalan Bandar Police Station spoke to him rapidly in Cantonese after they sat down on makeshift stools round an old wooden desk. A policeman in khaki shorts and grey shirt wearing a *songkok* stood nearby; other station officials walked freely in and out.

Ti Shuang kept his full lips pursed and sat erect as his aides briefed Dahlan on the events leading to the arrest of Ti Shuang and twenty-eight of his followers. Some of the men and women, all in white, were staring at Dahlan through the bars of their cell some four metres away. Ti Shuang wouldn't hear of bail. Some of his followers, one of them a fourteen-year-old girl, couldn't raise the five hundred dollars needed and he was not prepared to move out before she did. When he got back to his office with the aides, Dahlan rang up his friend, Inspector Swaran Singh, who said somewhat quickly that he had nothing to do with the case.

Dahlan said, "Just one thing you tell me, uh. Why have you arrested them. They were simply praying in the open air."

Swaran Singh said, "Ay, your fellow is the founder of some sort of cult, you know."

Dahlan said, "Why are you using the wrong words, don't use the wrong words. Want to say they pray in their own way, say so, man. Just like you pray in your own way. What's wrong with that?" For some reason he did not add just like I pray in mine.

Swaran Singh spoke placatingly, "Nothing's wrong with that. But I ask you, you remember what happened in Mercang?"

"That has got nothing to do with this."

Swaran Singh said, "Those fellows also were praying in their way, what did they do? Raided the Police Station after that and slashed everyone. One was a woman seven months pregnant, you know. Also *mati*, ha-ah."

Dahlan spoke slowly, "My fellows are not like that, Swaran."

"How to tell?" Swaran came back. "They all start praying together, then they close their eyes and shake about—you know, how do you say, sway from one side to another side. Next thing what happens—everyone else is their enemy. The buggers lose their senses, I tell you. You should see them."

Dahlan said, "Come on, man, not a single one of my fellows carried any weapon. They were all dressed in white—"

"The Mercang fellows also the same."

"Wait a minute, let me finish. They were all dressed in white, they were kneeling in the rain. In the mud. Just—just—tell me, what do you guys suppose they were going to do like that?"

Swaran Singh said he had better not say any more. He said he thought the charge was going to be illegal assembly, and he rang off.

• • •

Dahlan held Ti Shuang's sallow-faced aide with his eyes for a few moments and said, "Are you telling me the truth. Tell me the whole story again."

They drove to the site where the arrests were made. Beyond the outskirts of the city they passed several makeshift motor workshops on either side of the road. Where private houses appeared, there were plank and zinc structures with wire netting for fences as if to keep in poultry. The grass verge on both of the road was uneven and bare in several places; though trees cast their shade, the area looked unverdant, unkempt. When they stopped seven kilometres out of the city it took Dahlan a few minutes to realise that the vast junkyard before them was in fact the prayer site. Along one boundary empty oil barrels lay on their sides piled neatly in high triangular accumulations. Along another were heaps of rusting crankcases, cylinder heads and other parts of car engines, and piles of bent reinforcing steel rods. The junkyard was some one-and-a-half metres lower than the road level, and a culvert under the road had poured debris and refuse onto the flat, sandy ground. The greater part of the yard was an open area of red laterite that had been washed by rain many times over.

The entrance was marked by a six-metre-tall bamboo pole held upright by a trestle of short beams. At the top of the pole flew a banner with Chinese characters imprinted on it in red. Two rows of man-size burned-out joss sticks lined a pathway. At the far end was a dilapidated hut that served as a small prayer hall. There were the familiar brass urn, burning joss sticks, and fruit and flowers: but no images. It was on the desolate patch surrounding this hall that the faithful gathered on that rainy night to pray, the soggy laterite sticking to their shoes and soiling their clothes, the two aides told Dahlan.

"They brought the riot police, you know. Dogs also," the man said. "The OCPD spoke something, most of us could not hear him and did not understand him. Ti Shuang walked up and we knelt in prayer, singing our holy song. We did not resist. Then Ti Shuang led the elders to the police vans. Some of the congregation also joined them."

Not long after that, Dahlan was not sure what he had hoped to achieve by addressing no one in particular on the topic of religious intolerance from the steps of St. Peter's Church in Malacca. To the plainclothes men who interviewed him in the Special Branch Office in Kiang, he said it had nothing to do with Ti Shuang's movement. He denied he was a communist, or a socialist. He shook his head wearily at the suggestion that he was *kafir*.

Gita who pressed him to tell her what had happened at the interview said, bitterly, "I too am *kafir*. Better not be with me, *abang*." She was nervous from the moment he returned from the interview.

He said, exasperatedly, "How many times must I tell you, don't fall for their talk. They don't really mean it."

She said, "Tell me something. Why are you wasting your time on such things. Speaking like that. Bring trouble on yourself only."

They argued some more but she was hostile where he wanted reassurance in the path he had chosen.

He said, "All of us must make amends. Each and every one of us has to make an individual effort. Words are not enough. We must show by individual actions that we will not tolerate bigotry and race hatred."

She said, "Have you thought that your actions may only fan such feelings?"

"It is because we didn't face such feelings before, that May 13th happened."

She said, "Look at the way you're doing it. You think anyone cares what you do?"

He said, "It will give people heart."

She said, "They'll only think you a fool. I tell you, you cannot save these people simply by standing up and talking. Want to talk, at least talk before some proper people. Who were there to hear you? You told me: a few hawkers who didn't understand you, and some teenagers. What's the use?"

He was stung by her scorn. He said, "You don't care."

"I care. But you do these grand things like a hero—it's so easy. Have you thought about us? Now that's hard. That you won't dare."

He said, "What do you mean?"

"You know what I mean." Her face was pale, her eyes glistened.

Very hesitantly, he put an arm round her shoulders. "I think about us all the time."

She said, "I'm tired, *abang*. I don't know where we are."

When he held her, she realised that it was not passion alone that moved him, but curiously, a remorse in his tenderness that made her burst out weeping.

He continued to work late in the office trying to escape the thought: I am fooling no one but myself in thinking I can change anything.

6

From black the sky turned a smudged dark blue and the night chill began to wear off. A motorcycle went past, the tinny whine of its engine breaking the early morning quiet. A car followed at great speed. The vast newly-built suburb around throbbed as though in twenty thousand houses people had awakened, and were revving motorcycle and car engines. Minibuses and buses added a rising drone to the sounds of the suburb which now pressed in waves on the roofs, against the walls of the houses of the middle-class people in the earliest of the projects carried out in the city. Far away were the hills, the sides of some of them scoured red where the trees had been felled and brush cleared for another development scheme.

In Yun Ming's apartment it was still quiet, except for the sounds of the suburb that leaked in and echoed. The pale light of the morning coming in through the shuttered windows fell uncertainly over Yun Ming's face where he had sat motionless for more than four hours. He heard his neighbour drag up the phlegm in his throat with a grating sound. A radio played the beat of a Roberta Flack song sung in Cantonese. Twenty thousand radios carried the same beat, the same popular singer's voice. The single electric light cast a yellow line on his shoes, socks and shirt that had been flung carelessly on the sitting room floor.

Once when the suburb consisted only of the first phase of its growth, the house had been noisier and gayer. Phyllis and, later, their son, Chye, were there then. Phyllis never called their son Chye, but William. That was one of their quarrels. Now they were gone, only Chye's toys which Phyllis had left behind, which lay cluttered on the dresser; and the Brer Rabbit drawings and the magazine pictures of animals gummed on pasteboard to remind him—"of a previous existence," he said to himself.

"It's funny the way you *kow tow*," Phyllis once said, after they returned from an official dinner. "There was that silly little man talking such rubbish, and you kept saying, 'Yes, Datuk', 'No, Datuk'." If she had smiled when she said it, it would have made a difference, Yun Ming thought. She would make other remarks in the same way. When he started to make a half-hearted defence, she snapped, "Don't talk to me about the need to understand one another. That's what you were going to say, isn't it?" The weather was too much for her: she had frequent headaches and took Valium at night to sleep. Yun Ming was surprised how easily he lost the desire for her. He had a short-lived affair with a cocktail lounge hostess in the city until Phyllis discovered it and said she wanted to go home: she would take Chye with her and get a divorce in England. The cocktail lounge hostess was a convenient excuse Phyllis seized upon;

actually it was the country she had tired of. Despite her pleas, Yun Ming was not prepared to go back with her to England. He doggedly maintained a loyalty to his country that seemed forced to her.

Yun Ming missed Chye badly. His father too was furious that Yun Ming had let the boy go. Chye would be up every morning, making funny gurgling sounds, looking at a picture book propped against his knees. Now Chye had gone away and surely would not be back. Without him Yun Ming didn't like being in the house and only returned at night to sleep.

Last night he had not slept at all. He had returned at four in the morning, switched on a solitary light in the sitting room, taken off his shirt and shoes, and flung them on the floor. Then he had sat, in a singlet, on the long, cushioned seat that ran along the wall, staring into the air. His arm ached, his mouth was dry, he felt again the sweat of their embrace. The house suddenly shook with the sounds of rifle-shots outside; voices were raised; a car screeched, then seemed to shift gears at great speed, and moved away.

Yun Ming, startled, shook of the sleeplessness of the night before and picked up the telephone. If Omar answered, he would concoct something.

"Hullo." It was Sara.

"There's some trouble in my area. I was worried."

She said, "I'm all right. Are you okay?"

"Yes."

"You shouldn't call here." She wasn't angry.

"I know."

She asked, "Have you packed?"

"Yes. No."

"What time is your flight?"

"Ten. I can make it." He hung up.

What had happened? He couldn't go to the beginning, he didn't know where it was. He could not start at the end. *This was not the end, it could not be the end.* He sat down again on the long, cushioned seat leaning his head against the wall, and stretched his leg out. Somewhere in the angsana tree which he had planted in his garden, came the trilling notes from the magpie robin which was there every morning. A mynah replied with a short tremolo, a game response to an unbeatable challenger. After they stopped, he heard again the low and continuing melodious gurgle of the bulbuls, as if they were all talking at the same time, and all understanding and agreeing with each other too. Once a bulbul had flown straight into his windowpane and fallen stunned on the ledge outside. He had picked it up and given it a drink of water. It shook its head and fluffed its feathers and its tiny legs buckled a bit.

Then as he watched, it fluttered its wings and flew unsteadily to the nearest branch of the angsana tree.

• • •

Her car had stopped behind his along a high ridge, and both had switched their lights off. Ahead of them the road climbed further for about two hundred yards, becoming more potholed and eventually ending without any destination just below the top of the hill. Tall structures, probably electric pylons, held out gaunt metallic arms in the dark as if in a silhouetted Balinese dance. To their left the land swung sharply downwards and into the darkness where the *lallang* rustled. The jagged branches of a small cherry tree rising out of the incline created a canopy through which the bluish light of a distant street lamp filtered. The lights of the house nearest to them were out. He sat quietly for more than a minute to confirm that the spot was deserted. Then he left his car, opened her door and sat in the seat next to her.

She looked at him, then he turned her shoulders towards him and kissed her. Her body shook in small spasms in his embrace. She marveled that his roughness was no longer there, and wished she had worn her usual *sarong kebaya* instead of a full-length western-style dress. Suddenly he released her and said, "What are you wearing, a coat of mail?" They broke into suppressed laughter and kissed again, still laughing. Then she grew strangely silent and he turned away. She was absolutely still when he looked at her again. The tight neck of her dress was slightly awry, the sleeves appeared loosed at the shoulders. She looked at him and still said nothing.

"He said, "Don't say anything."

She said, "We are mad." Her eyes were closed. He was kissing her violently now and she felt a surge of answering passion and her whole frame shuddered.

They saw the lights of a car coming up the lane and were still. The reflected beams lighted up their figures momentarily and then veered off as the car went the other way.

She said, "You're going tomorrow."

"I suppose so. You are, too."

She was silent a long time. He looked in her eyes and could not fathom their shining depth. She held his gaze unwaveringly until at last he cast his eyes down.

She said, "You must go."

"I waited for you for so long."

"We shouldn't stay here. Anyone will come."

He said, "Can I see you again?"

"When? You're going overseas."

"Sara, you're going too. The night I first saw you, you were so beautiful, I simply wanted to hold you there and then. It seemed just the natural thing to do. We didn't have to talk, we didn't have to go through any formalities. We just simply had to get together. Did you feel like that? Just a little bit? Sara?"

He looked into her eyes which shone, whether in assent or otherwise he did not know. Her gaze was steady. There was a hint of a smile in her features but he couldn't say where exactly. The serenity of her countenance disconcerted him. Still she did not speak.

He pulled her roughly to him. He said, "Come to my place", and felt her loose against him. He drove on the deserted road, her head resting on his shoulder. The street lights winked past, the sky was moonless and banked with thick clouds. Soon after an open-air seafood restaurant they turned into a lane, the loud rapping sound of the ladle on the *wok*, and the aroma of frying garlic trailing them as they fled into their darkness.

They were on a silent shore and she called up to him and he pursued her with a frenzy when she swerved inland into a trackless forest. She ran through undergrowth, down a hill to where she could hear the flowing water of a river. The brown river sand felt soft under her feet and she approached a little cave out of which the waters of a spring trickled. Throats parched, they were bending to drink when a voice stopped her.

A man with stubble on his chin and wearing a black robe stood with his hand poised to throw a stone at her. She bent to drink from the spring but the water was brackish. The hill shook and they tumbled together, revelling in the freedom of their embrace and he said he loved her and she lay under him, her skin golden the way he first saw her the night of the cultural dances, and the wells of her eyes were at peace as she looked at him.

Suddenly she started, lifting her head, listening. "There's someone at the gate," she said.

He was motionless. "It's just a passer-by."

She turned on her side, her body taut, still listening. She said, "It's not safe."

He said, "There's nothing to fear, Sara, they don't come this way."

They lay for a while in silence until the tension left her limbs. Light from the passageway entered in a thin rectangle through a door not fully closed. From the window overlooking the road, vague illumination from the stars and even from the square of hawkers' stalls not far away spread over the floor and onto the bed.

She said, "You were hard on Vikram."

"I don't care."

"I never thought you could talk like that."

He said, "What do you mean?"

"You shook us all."

He unfolded a sheet and put it over them.

"Sara."

"Mm."

"Will you marry me?"

She stared. She said, "You don't have to say anything like that. It's not necessary. I understand. You have to go."

"I'm not making this up, do you believe me." But he knew he sounded false.

She disengaged herself, then suddenly leaned across and pressed her mouth softly against his. She said, "We'd better go."

She got up and began putting on her clothes; he tried to help her do the buttons at the back but fumbled. Putting her hands behind her, she swiftly completed the task. Then she sat near the window, her face impassive, its Balinese features and her hair silhouetted in profile against the faint light outside.

Above the desultory noise of the suburb the taxi's diesel engine clattered noisily. Inside the house, Yun Ming roused himself and brought his suitcase and attachè case out. To Ratnam, his grizzled, betel-red-toothed gardener he handed his house keys with instructions that he hand them to the landlord. The year before, Ratnam had come to his house asking for work. His shirt was stained irregularly brown, he wore tattered khaki trousers and dusty slippers. He had refused the dollar note Yun Ming had tried to send him off with and insistently asked for work. And when Yun Ming relented and hired him on a part-time basis, Ratnam's deep voice boomed out a melodious tune in thanks. Today, Ratnam's face was somber, his jaw covered in grey stubble ajar as if about to ask a question. He stood clutching the keys awkwardly in front of him as he watched the taxi depart.

The streets were littered with rubbish. A few cars overtook the taxi at great speed. At a bus-stop, people who were clambering roughly on to a bus, suddenly scattered in all directions. A soldier had leaped out of a military jeep and dragged one of the passengers out of the bus. "Why, why, I haven't done anything. What for?" the passenger was screaming in Cantonese as he was dragged away. The taxi wheeled into a lane and seemed to be lost in a maze of side streets. To Yun Ming's suppressed exclamation, the taxi driver said, "What for go to Federal Highway? Still got fighting. Damansara Utama better for you."

At first, guests had tried to overcome the awkwardness they felt at being placed next to strangers during dinner by talking about occupations, incomes and places of residence. More animated talk followed on local politics, the share market situation, or the private life of a prominent figure. At one or two tables, the guests were lucky to be able to garner choice bits of information from old hands from a Ministry or a boardroom.

They had eaten the barbecued lamb, the grilled steaks and the green lettuce. Through crispy, aromatic smoke which spread thinly across the flood-lit lawn, they had picked at the *satay* with their teeth and sipped glasses of wine and beer. Loud laughter frequently burst forth from a few tables followed by moments of unnatural quiet. The talk at one table was about a bomb explosion outside the house of Wan Nurudin, Secretary-General to Housing Minister a few days previously. His gate was blasted open; a security guard killed. That's why the dinner was being held at Panglima's house and Wan Nurudin, though present, was in the background. The lady who provided the details, Esther Fu, had plucked eyebrows which had been painted over in two semicircular black lines. The semicircles moved up and down when she spoke. That's what she had heard. She explained that there had been a top-level meeting: a new policy towards the disorder in the town had been drafted. "You'll see," she said. "We'll soon be able to walk safely in the streets."

"It's true isn't it, Panglima," Esther Fu turned to her neighbour, but Panglima was talking with the host, Wan Nurudin, who had left his seat and was directing a waiter towards a circle of guests who had stood up after the meal. Panglima's lips smiled; his eyes glowered behind the thick frames of his spectacles.

He had enlisted Sara soon after she arrived to help his wife welcome the guests. Yun Ming was talking with Dr. Wahab from the University of Technology when the voice of a guest rose above the hubbub of conversation.

"But tell me, uh, is this a promotion?" Another guest replied, "Posted to Bangkok, sure what, that's a promotion." The laughter that followed was loud and forced.

"Now he can live in a free house, have servants, chauffeur, mistresses—any number also can."

Yun Ming said, "I think I will enjoy Thai culture and its history the most. The wars, the Buddhas, the arts."

"Uh-huh." Everyone laughed again.

Dr. Wahab said, "Whatever you may say, it's a reward for faithful service."

"What's the difference between faithful service and ball carrying?" The words came from Vikram Toh who had been silent for most of the evening. His cheeks were slightly flushed, his speech slurred. On his pockmarked face, the lips widened in a slight smile. He had recently retired from the Foreign Service and was bitter that he had never been appointed ambassador. The others turned to him recognising from the tone of his voice that a familiar last phase in open-air barbecue parties in the capital was about to commence. The poor attempts at jokes which provoked the laughter of persons who were unsure of themselves ceased. Now without warning a chord was touched and everyone felt the friction in the air waiting for the evening to take on a different hue, where two persons would converse and the rest listened.

Silence had followed the remark. Dr. Wahab looked straight ahead. Esther Fu glanced at Yun Ming, her fingers nervously tapping the table. Vikram spoke again. "No, come on. No need to be shy. No harm admitting the truth; you were a very good boy. The question is, what about the other bit?"

"Other bit?"

"You know." Vikram made a gesture with one hand, pointing his thumb and two fingers upwards, and moved them up and down a few times. "Call it the working hard after office hours bit. Patpong on the house. Hurray."

Esther said, "You never became ambassador."

Someone said, "He did."

"Oh yes, once. The hardship post. Nigeria, was it? Togo?"

Yun Ming held Vikram with his eyes for some moments. Then he said, "Have another drink."

Vikram drained his glass and slapped it back on the table for it to be refilled. He addressed the guests at large. "Now here's a guy, when he was in university, you would never have said he was going to be an ambassador one day. Champion ragger. My God, some of the things he did. He and who was that other fellow, Dahlan. Suddenly he changed. All of a sudden so serious."

"That was after May 13th."

"All of us changed after that."

Vikram said, "Yah, but not the way this bugger changed." Someone said, "I remember that fellow Prasad. Engineering Department. Don't know what came over him. He used to go around with two cronies threatening to report people who didn't speak Malay in the house."

"I think he became a little *gila*."

Vikram said, "*Gila*, don't talk. He was on all sorts of committees. Powerful, you know. And he made you remember it."

Yun Ming said, "One thing's for sure. Vikram remained the same, May 13th or no May 13th. Shamsuddin can vouch for that, I'm sure."

"Shamsuddin?"

"You know. The Ministry driver. The one who goes for the four digits."

Vikram said, "What about him?"

"Do you remember seeing him in Chow Kit? During the May 13th time?"

Dr. Wahab said, shaking his head, "That was a bad area."

Esther said, "Some soldiers, uh, they came into Chow Kit, make it only worse. Started shooting for nothing. People just running home scared also, they shoot."

Vikram said, "The soldiers came later."

Yun Ming said, "That's right. After the trouble started, the Chinese were out for revenge. Many Malays were killed that night and the next morning."

Esther said, "I know a Chinese family there. They hid a Malay couple, you know. Three days. Only place was under the bed. Food also they had to eat under the bed. But the husband, uh, he died, you know. Foolish, I tell you. The family told him, don't go out, the gangs are searching for Malays, he don't want to listen. Second day he went downstairs and ran out on the street to try to get back to Kampung Bahru. No use. They found his body the next day."

Dr. Wahab said, "Other Chinese families also hid Malays."

The noise and chatter from the neighbouring tables seemed to recede far away into the night. At this table, the people instinctively huddled, startled that facades had broken open. They reached to each other as they spoke, fearful that what was in their hearts would be known to the others or that the cold, remorseless night air would drag out the bitterness from where it lay hidden in the layers of their consciousness. Furtive glances never met eyes. Each was an exposed individual as well as a startled spectator. Postures, and words and even silences, suddenly became indicators of feelings that coursed in the blood. Their beings seemed to exude into the air some monstrous thing that was commonly their own, and awoke in them feelings of shame, relief and despair.

They no longer heard the loud voices of the other guests. They were the only guests, not only in the house, but it seemed in the whole dark universe and the night swooping down on them confirmed they were in a thrall.

Yun Ming's voice floated at them, "Shamsuddin was unlucky. No one to hide him. He only went to buy some cakes in Chow Kit and couldn't get back. He hid in a stinking monsoon drain for about five hours. A few cars went by driven by Chinese people, he didn't dare to stop them. Then he saw your car and because you look like a Malay he tried to stop you for a lift."

Vikram whispered, "What was happening in the streets that night, no one could have stopped."

"True man. It was terrible, wasn't it? When people were going mad everywhere, what could you do? You couldn't stop to help a fellow human being, could you? So Shamsuddin ran back to his dirty drain. Lucky for him the soldiers came."

Esther said, "Not so lucky for others, man."

Vikram's voice was trembling. "Why are you saying all this? I never saw Shamsuddin before he joined the Ministry as a driver."

Yun Ming said, "He remembered your car number. Any car he has anything to do with, he memorises the number. He didn't win a prize with your number, but it stuck, and when he saw you driving, he remembered."

Vikram's eyes were glistening. He said, "I never heard such rubbish."

Yun Ming stood up and said, "Talking about balls, you never had any, Vikram." He held Vikram with a fixed smile for a while. "To be carried. Or for anything."

Dr. Wahab got up and mumbled, "*Alamak*, I didn't know it was so late."

Esther said, "I must look for husband. Well, it's been nice meeting you. Goodbye. Goodbye, Yun Ming, and the best of luck. Goodbye. Nice seeing you. Goodbye. Goodbye."

The tension disappeared, it had begun to loosen even before she left Panglima's house. Following the car in front of her, and studying now the silhouette, now the part profile, of its driver's head, hardly aware of the danger of the darkened road, aware only of the chill of the night air, she knew something like inner excitement. Excitement that moved her stomach like a pang of hunger. It set her face in a fixed stare on the rear lights of the car ahead, its amber indicator lights blinking left, and left, and then right.

Images played in her mind; words interrupted then often. The table at which she was a silent presence; the apologetic glances at her during references to May 13th; the garden spotlight that put Vikram's face into partial shade when he turned away from it; Yun Ming's words, uttered without emotion. She was in the States when May 13th happened. In a pizza shop, in fact, with her house mates. On the small black and white television screen, she saw some people chasing others; a car overturned, some bodies lying inert on the road and heard the news of the outbreak of violence in Kuala Lumpur.

After the initial panic when she had called home and learned that Omar and her parents were safe, she had subsided into an attitude of expectancy in the quiet of her room, her mind threading its way through garbled excerpts of news. She was waiting for the sense that would tell her that people had begun living again. She pondered over the uses of words like 'disturbances', 'trouble', 'riots' and 'killing', noting how the use of each unerringly identified the user. She entered into some defensive arguments with her American friends over whether Malays were killing Chinese and Indians, or vice versa. It was all because of economic backwardness, she said, realising in the same breath that she had said more than she meant to. She added that, after all, we are building a new country, we were working out our own future and we will solve our problems as they arise. She developed and clung to the use of the plural personal pronoun because they soothed her: they stirred feelings of patriotism, of love for fellow citizens whether Malay, Chinese, Indian or Eurasian. They exempted her from asking what really had happened.

Tonight for the first time she knew that she had not really wanted to know: she had embraced a specious feeling of togetherness with people in the abstract to cloak her unease, to disguise her semi-instinctive wish not to know.

Yun Ming knew. This evening his head was less inclined, his fixed deferential manner which previously repelled her had vanished. His face was unsmiling, his voice grated like leather. One of the garden spotlights shone nearly full on him: he looked like a snake that had sloughed off a skin. She watched the way he leaned over the table and saw his tongue darting, his eyes, pinpoints of black, flash in the light as he spoke.

They mesmerised her: she knew he spoke as one who knew. She tried to hold him with her eyes, but though he turned in her direction now and then, and looked deep into her eyes, he looked through her. She craved reassurance.

The car in front of her had turned into a deserted road, amber indicator lights blinking left again. Though no words had passed between them, she knew she was doing his bidding. Tall angsana trees lining the road on either side created a womb-like darkness, a tunnel through which they trailed quietly, headlights off. She stopped behind his car on the low darkened ridge overlooking the winking lights of the city. She said to herself: I will speak to him just this once. After all, he is going away.

Sara picked up the receiver knowing, though it was impossible, that it was Yun Ming.

He said, "Hi, it's me."

She said, "But you're supposed to have gone. Where are you calling from?"

"Penang. The airport. I have two hours here. What are you doing?"

"I have a lecture in a few minutes."

He said, "I was in a shop a few moments ago. Guess what I bought? I bought something for you."

"What?"

"A set of press-studs."

"What? What for?" She stopped and suppressed a giggle.

"How can I get them to you?"

She said, facetiously, "You can always bring them to me personally."

"Shall I?"

He was serious, she thought with wonder. And then she realised, she was, too. They were deliberately unbinding layers of the past.

He was speaking again. "Shall I? I want to see you again. I cannot go without seeing you again."

But how, she said to herself. She had classes that day and then on Friday she was going with Omar to Jerangau to start a new life.

They were silent for a long time, sharing with each other the exhilaration of being child-like.

He said, "Are you going to live in Jerangau?"

"Yes."

"Do you think you might come back from time to time."

She said, "No. I don't know."

"There could be trouble there, too, I heard. Will you be careful?"

"Yes."

"Do you think we might—do you think—"

She was straining her ears to catch his words. Softly, he said, "I have to go now. Goodbye."

"Goodbye."

7

AFTER SETAPAK ON the edge of the city; rows of dilapidated wooden shops and houses appeared. Their plank walls which kept out both rain and heat showed dark patches of decay. The zinc roofs had rusted maroon, the metal sheets lay askew. After the road took an inexplicable right-hand curve, the highway suddenly branched out from it, heading straight towards the central mountain range that lay across its path in layers of receding blue.

At a sentry box a few hundred metres on, three men in army fatigues, M-16s slung on their shoulders, waved them down.

Sara looked at Omar and sat still. Omar leaning across said, "Lucky thing it's our people. I was thinking at first I should turn back."

One of the soldiers said, "Step out." He checked their identity cards and then stood guard while his two companions searched the car.

"Where are you going?"

"Jerangau."

"Travel pass."

Omar looked inquiringly.

The soldier said again, "Travel pass."

Omar said, "Haven't got. I didn't know it's needed."

The soldier said, "To Pahang or Jerangau means must have travel pass."

The two soldiers examined the boot of the car and came back. They spoke among themselves for a few minutes.

The first soldier said, "Don't take the new road, there's trouble in Kampung Beladau there. Go by the old road."

"Thanks."

"Next time get a travel pass."

In the lowland on the either side, there was scrub and sparse secondary undergrowth; occasionally over a neat, dark-green vegetable patch a bare-backed farmer bent tending the soil. Beyond that a new housing estate stretched out, rows of uniform white-walled houses on a treeless, laterite plain. Ahead, the chalky-coloured limestone hills rose perpendicularly amidst hills scraped clear of bush and undergrowth, looking like sharply bruised whitened flesh in the seconds before the blood begins to flow.

Omar said, "I heard the army is going to have another big operation. Don't know where."

Sara was tired. She wore no makeup and her skin was pale. She said, "I hope it's not in Jerangau."

Omar said, "Never. Most likely north side—Raub, places like that." After a while he said, "As if things are not bad, that fellow Dahlan wants to make it worse."

"You mean his talk in front of the church?"

"That. Also defending those cult followers. He acts like he's the only one who knows anything."

The road began to wind up the mountain range. The bends were graceful as if they had mastered the style of ascent needed. Occasionally the cut was so steep so that the hewn sides of the excavated hill rose sheer thirty metres on either side, and for a few kilometres in either direction the road was splattered with orange mud.

They were passing through rubber estates now, the rows of shady trees giving the impression of a forest. The air became suddenly cooler. Straight ahead loomed a solitary peak, thin, craggy and vaguely menacing.

Who could she talk to?

Gita maybe. Now it was too late. But then she had never in the past confided details of her personal life to Gita, and Gita had not shown any curiosity either. It was more like respect. What Gita could not understand she did not probe. Even when she heard that Sara was resigning as lecturer suddenly, there was an exclamation of astonishment and then, quickly, a muted response.

Sara reiterated that she was going with her husband to Jerangau. "I'm sorry I couldn't tell you before. There was so much to do."

Gita's eyes reddened. "What am I going to do?"

Sara said, "It's better to go to a quiet place and live one's own life. You're often said that too." She wondered whether Gita might think her words insincere. It was by words that she was judged.

"But—your students?"

Sara was going to say in mock self-deprecation, "I think they'll miss me a lot" when she remembered Wah Loong.

Gita said, "Will you write?"

"I will. I don't know."

Gita tried some of her familiar banter that had always been their private verbal code. She became silent after that, even aloof. Her farewell was stilted, as if she were speaking to a stranger.

Omar had said that in the north she would rediscover the beauty of her religion which had been looked upon with scorn by foreigners. When he came back from his tour in the Middle East she had ignored the accents of inspired passion with which he spoke. She had not tried to understand him. She had even experienced fear listening to him speak, looking at his transformation which had occurred overnight. She had become so used to easy ways, to following impulse, that she had forgotten what was her own, and had failed to recognise it even when it was presented to her. She had lost discipline, she had deviated. Now she would return to the true path.

The road was rising steeply but Omar didn't lessen speed. Approaching the crest above which banks of darkening clouds rose like a giant cinema screen, it seemed they could only shoot straight upwards from the crest into the grey sky. Then they were descending rapidly with cool forest on the hills on either side. The lines of vegetation formed by clusters of branches created a balance of melodic shades of green, and you could tell that the air was still after rain by the mist which tapered upwards in places in neat, motionless patches of white.

The forest gave way to secondary jungle. On a cleared space by the side of the road a yellow signboard with black lettering said, 'Sin Min Engineering Works'. Two men in stained tee-shirts and jeans bent over the hulk of a blackened car engine under a zinc-roofed shed without walls. They were approaching a small town: on the road were a few cyclists and some people dressed in workaday clothes. Further on, a row of ramshackle wooden shophouses fronted by a red laterite open space came into view. By the road's edge, occasionally, flame of the forest trees, not yet in bloom, cast uncertain shade. It was a typical small town and its rows of wooden shops on either side of the road for a space of a hundred metres did not quite dissipate its rural air, protected as it was by distance and natural vegetation from the disturbances of the cities. But its peacefulness had been shattered: in a gap in the row of shacks were the charred remains of two houses, their blackened wooden supports pointing futilely to the sky. A car with two flat tyres and shattered windscreen stood in front.

They cruised past a newly built row of shops with individual Minangkabau roofs. Omar was looking for a *mee rebus* stall. There were coffeeshops and provision shops. Outside, some bananas hung in combs, almost completely screening the inside of the shop from view. Oranges, duku, apples and papayas lay spread out in sloping patches of orange, brown, green, red and yellow. Omar finally chose the food shop at the end of the row.

A Chinese family of six sat round one table silently levering rice to their mouths with chopsticks and picking food from the dishes laid out on the table. Apart from pausing fleetingly, they paid no attention to the Malay couple who had just entered but Omar knew the family were aware of them.

"No, *encik*," the matronly woman who ran the place said in broken Malay to Omar. They didn't have *mee rebus*, "Why not try other things? Fried *mee hoon* got, fried rice got. *Sotong*." She trailed off looking expectantly. She had on a faded *samfoo*, the trousers rolled up to her calves. "Everything here is *halal*, you know. I can make for you very fast." Her plain, fat, friendly daughter took their order. The clatter of plates and the sound of the metal ladle on the wok from the dark kitchen at the back sounded loud in the silence of the surrounding hills.

He said, "There is nothing and nobody here for us to recognise as our own. When I went overseas, then only I realised what we had lost. Dahlan acts as if we have lost nothing."

She thought: Dahlan is doing something different. She said, "Maybe he doesn't know it."

"Huh. He has forgotten who he is."

Impulsively she wanted to contradict him. But what was the point. She was leaving welter behind.

She said, "He is an attraction. People are eager to hear someone talking so freely."

He interrupted her. "It's not that. He thinks he's so brave. He wants to be a hero. He sees what is happening to this place and yet he has the heart to make more trouble."

"He is saying what they want to hear. They love to watch him, they're fascinated. I think he knows he can't last."

She watched his eyes redden and, when they were in the car again and the little town was left far behind, his knuckles tightened round the steering wheel, his instinctive reaction to these alien surroundings. His shining directness demanded wholehearted commitment. She could see how in the past year fervent affirmation had simultaneously nurtured disgust for those beyond the pale.

The road was flatter and narrower now. Over long stretches the asphalt had loosened with repeated heavy rains and flooding, so that the car threw up gravel as it sped. This part of the country was full of fruit trees: rambutan, jackfruit and duku. The names of *kampungs* on neat, new signboards flashed past: Kampung Gaung, Kampung Telaga Mengkudu, Kampung Beras. At each signboard a narrow road branched away into secondary forest, sometimes roughly asphalted, sometimes just a sandy lane consisting of two continuous ruts which countless vehicles had scoured out and a ridge running along the middle, tufted with coarse grass. The lanes disappeared, it seemed, into the cool of the rubber estates and fruit orchards, secure from the venom that coursed on the streets of the major towns.

Here, in secluded places away from manipulation, were groups of families who lived near each other, their bonds as strong as they were unspoken. Houses stood in a cool haven, the sunlight through the thick branches of the fruit trees specking the scene with dancing spots of gold. Even on the edge of the road the raised wooden houses looked tranquil. In one makeshift structure on stilts, a bare-shouldered mother in a faded batik *sarong* and brassiere sat on the steps with a few children. They passed poor people, aged men who sat in verandahs looking vacantly at their gardens, pubescent girls in ragged *baju kurung*, older women with stumps of red betel in their mouths. Sara thought of darkness falling in the *kampung*: the *lorong* would only be sporadically illuminated by light that spilled onto it through the thick foliage from the sheltered dwellings along the way. It made her pensive.

Omar glanced at her and said, "You had forgotten."

She was silent.

He said, with sudden passion, "I hated those people in KL talking about freedom. Free for what? Just to deny our rights. Better we live our own way."

She had known him as a carefree undergraduate and then as a domineering husband. Now the single point of agreement with him turned out to be associated with the nerve of the Iranian tumult within him. Driving through the gloom of the rubber estates, she saw his mouth set, his eyes narrow and his head jut out over the steering wheel, and for the first time she was frightened of him.

He said, "We'll be all right. First we must purify and strengthen ourselves, then nothing can touch us. We'll be all right."

This was a manner he had begun to cultivate: rage was overcome by remembering that all obstacles would be removed, everything could be explained, everything fell into place in the vision he had and would impart to others when the time was ripe.

Suddenly it was late afternoon. The road was level, curving only gently every couple of miles. Emerging from the shady road along which they had driven, the open sky cast a heightened pallor on their faces. They were passing dry *padi* land now overgrown with *lallang* and weeds and extending far on either side of the road to the edge of rubber plantations in the distance. A few clumps of short trees stood out but the land looked deserted and unworked.

Omar said, "You know Yun Ming?"

She looked out of the window.

"Yun Ming. Posted to Bangkok. He gave you a lift home after the concert."

She didn't react.

"He tried to understand. How many people understand?"

She said, "There are many others."

"I don't think so."

"My students. Gita."

"That's nothing. Even they—"

She said, "Even outside. Many ordinary people show respect and understanding. We should do the same to them."

"It's their duty. They came here as strangers, they must show their understanding of the situation. I doubt if they're sincere. Even those who seem to be trying, like Yun Ming—they cannot be trusted."

"Why?"

He said, "He's too sympathetic to Dahlan."

"They were in university together."

"That's why. That's Yun Ming. Though he may want to change he likes to remember the past. Even though the past is a disgrace to him. I know why. After all that's when his father became rich."

"Have you talked to him about it?"

He said, "Long time ago, we were at a *muhibah* party. Soon after May sixty-nine. That's the first time I met him. Already he could speak Malay so fluently. He's not Baba. His father came from China. I remember thinking maybe here's just another Chinese saying many words about cooperation and harmony. I didn't go there to listen to those kind of words. I just wanted to see which Chinese would come. I just wanted to see their faces after what happened. I just wanted to get from them whatever we could—food and money, mainly. The Chinese had those things in the past and never shared with anyone, now they must share. At that time many young men were like me: Chinese—all Chinese are rich and I envied them.

Before, they couldn't care less about you. You should have seen them at the party. Bowing, smiling, saying '*encik*'. So hypocritical. All the time they were trying to see how to get favours, now that at last we were in charge. Yun Ming wasn't like that. He spoke little, he offered to help at the relief centre... What's the matter?"

She wiped her eyes with the fingers of one hand, resting the hand lightly on the cheekbone in a covering gesture after that. "It's nothing. Just some dust."

Nobody could get May sixty-nine right, she thought. It was hopeless to pretend you could be objective about it. Speaking even to someone close to you, you were careful for fear the person might unwittingly quote you to others. If a third person was present, it was worse, you spoke for that person's benefit. If he was Malay you spoke one way, Chinese another way, Indian another. Even if he wasn't listening. In the end the spun tissue, like an unsightly scab, became your vision of what happened: the wound beneath continued to run pus.

Omar had never spoken like this before. She wondered whether he knew how much he was revealing about himself. Like the office driver who said to her, "*Masa 'tu hebat, kak. Saya masuk operasi jolok manggis. Banyak dapat.*"

There was here exulting power from which she recoiled.

He said, "I made friends with Yun Ming. He was willing to listen. I mean, sincerely. You remember those first days after the army came in?"

She said, "I was in the States. I saw pictures on TV. I didn't know what to do."

"Everyone in their houses, curfew on most of the time, and food running out. At the relief centre the big Chinese *towkays* brought their rice, tinned stuff and so on. I could see them. They were not just giving. They wanted something in return. Honours, opportunities, contracts, who knows? Yun Ming's father also brought things. Yun Ming went with the van taking goods for distribution to Malay areas. The trouble was not yet over, but he insisted on going. Two long trips every day. Dangerous. I think he started to see things differently from that time. That is why we became friendly. Long after that I heard he often went to *kampungs*, mostly in Malacca—he made a lot of friends. Right up to the end he was going. Just before he left also he went—" He paused and looked intently at the road ahead, his brow furrowed, "He went to Sayong, about the same time you were there. Did you see him?"

"What?"

"Did you see him in Sayong?"

"I was passing the field station. I saw him there." He held the steering wheel steady, his face now expressionless.

She said, "I was returning home after visiting Safiah and her family."

"In Lubok Baya?"

"She had a hard life. Five children, now the husband is also not well." She saw the wrinkles on his forehead lessen and her tone became lighter. "I took her some food, also some batik. She was my old schoolmate. From Standard One to Four."

He almost interrupted her, "What did Yun Ming have to say?"

"He talked about the trouble at Lubok Baya after the breaking of the statues."

"Is that why he went up? But he had nothing to with it. Most of his visits used to be in the Malacca area."

He paused for Sara to speak. She said nothing.

At least he said, "I remember now, he was acting rather oddly for the past few weeks. His wife has left him. Gone back to England with the son. Now he's gone too. The Thailand posting is just right for him."

She was very pale. She wound down the car window a little and let the wind slip in.

A new bridge, painted white, spanned a wide river, its concrete arches between the supports shining in the sunlight. The car thumped over metal girders that were covered by a thin layer of asphalt. Half a metre below, the mud-brown waters of the Jerangau river flowed lazily past little homesteads sheltered by trees on the banks, some standing in startling patches of green grass. On the other side the river kept alongside the highway partly hidden by low undergrowth. Sometimes it turned away in a sharp curve, then came back. Swamp began to appear, stagnant pools of water with rough vegetation sprouting here and there and trees stripped bare of their foliage and often of their crown of branches. The swamp spread towards the trees on the far side. They passed one pool where the water, the colour of rust, was disturbed by occasional ripples caused by underwater creatures. Seeing the denuded tree trunks, one thin and tapering upwards for thirty metres, others with sheds of foliage, and one bending and branching out dominantly with unflowering parasitic plants attached, getting some idea of a primeval age, of heat and decay, Sara had momentarily a sense of futility and desolation.

She thought: I should have refused to come; there is nothing I can do now. And closed her eyes.

She awoke to the sound of the rapid beat of the car's wipers and the sound of rain falling in torrents creating a thunderous din on the roof. The road was dark and Omar was bobbing in his seat peering through the misted windscreen with the aid of headlights which seemed to meet an impenetrable white wall of water after five feet. In the wind which whistled in furious gusts the car rocked unsteadily, slowing to a crawl. He wiped the fog on the windscreen with a cloth but the rain water pouring down faster than the wipers could clear it away distorted everything outside into writhing figures on glass. The red and yellow lights of vehicles close in front melted on the windscreen like jelly.

"Is this the place?"

He said, "I think we missed the turning."

Going back part of the way he found a *lorong* on the right into which he swung the car. The sound of the rain ceased as if it had been switched off. They were in a winding lane wide enough for only one car, overhung with the branches of trees which lined it closely.

Straddling the entire road, the car bumped over the rough asphalt, under showers of raindrops occasionally scattered by branches suddenly shaken by gusts of wind. They stopped at a wooden elevated house where a single yellow electric light shone weakly in the open verandah and sounded the car horn. After a while, a barebodied man in a *sarong* stepped out under an umbrella held by a woman; a boy stood on the verandah watching them.

Omar said, "Tok Guru Bahaudin. Is he here?"

The man said, "Tok Guru is not here."

"I am Omar. He knows I'm coming."

The man said nothing: he was looking at Omar without any expression, then at Sara, then into the back of their car.

Omar said, "Are you Bakar?"

Bakar said, "Where are you from?"

"Kuala Lumpur."

"Many people coming from the town."

Omar said again, "Tok Guru Bahaudin knows I am coming. We are going to live in Jerangau. This is my wife."

Bakar said, "Tok Guru has gone out. He didn't tell me anything."

"Where has he gone? He told us to come and stay in his house."

Bakar said nothing.

"Okay, then we have no choice. Don't mind, we will stay outside here until he comes back."

Bakar spoke a few words to the woman beside him. Then he said, "You have left Kuala Lumpur?"

"Yes."

"Are you going back?"

"We came to live here."

After a few moments the man said, "Tok Guru didn't say anything." He led them upstairs into the house.

They sat awkwardly in the open verandah on cushioned chairs covered with shiny plastic. With the closed windows there was a faintly musty air about the room. Bakar withdrew and emerged shortly afterwards wearing a *baju Melayu* and a white skull cap. He had a thin moustache and stubble on his chin; his face was red with erupted acne boils. His wife brought them glasses of green syrup water, the boy whose name was Rahman stared at them from a window.

Bakar said, "I have to be careful. There are some government people about. Special Branch."

Omar asked, "Has there been any trouble here?"

Bakar said, "You cannot go to Jerangau yet. I don't know when Tok Guru will come back. He has some matters to attend to. You can stay with us for a few days. Have you eaten?"

His wife laid out some cold rice, *sambal tumis* and fried fish. They ate hungrily without relish. Bakar left them alone after showing them the room they were to stay in.

Omar walked through the house and Sara walked behind him. On the walls hung portraits of bearded men wearing *jubah*, a picture of the Kabah and a reproduction in gold lettering of a lengthy Arabic inscription. Along a central darkened passage, Omar opened doors on either side. Two were bedrooms. In the one they were to occupy for the night they saw an old iron bedstead with a crumpled stained white sheet and a coloured woollen blanket half spreading out from the bed on the wooden floor. The window was shut and above it the frosted glass pane let in very little light. On a low dressing table with an oval mirror was a small Sony tape-recorder and some cassette tapes in an untidy pile. Sara looked at her reflection in the mirror and grimaced. Omar idly pressed a key and a recording commenced in mid-stream.

"*The best method of ruling the world is by a religious government. People say that* kafirs *will not agree with this but it is God's wish that this should be so. No doubt man lives by violence and he spills blood freely. But God has given man characteristics other creatures do not have. Man has the ability to govern everything. But has man used this ability? The answer is No. Man has failed to establish religion as the true guide for ruling the world. Instead religion has been put aside and we are plunged into the dark age of Western Secularism…*" Omar stopped the tape.

She went to the dressing table and looked at the titles of the other tapes.

Omar sped the machine fast forward and played it again.

"...*and no one will deny what is the meaning of treachery and betrayal,* khianat: *when man neglects his duty to set up a religious administration, then there is treachery and betrayal. Such abandonment is shameful...*"

He stopped the tape again when the door opened. Sara saw the boy Rahman, half hidden, peering in. She beckoned to him. He stepped in with exaggerated ease. He wore his *sarong* loosely draped from one shoulder, one arm resting on a fold as if in a sling.

Omar said, "In Kuala Lumpur you cannot get these tapes."

The boy said nothing. He came to the table and rearranged the tapes. Then began to fold up the blanket which had fallen to the floor.

Sara said, "Where is Tok Guru Bahaudin?"

Rahman spoke over his shoulder as he folded the blanket. "I don't know."

Omar said, "Rahman we've come to see Tok Guru Bahaudin."

"He'll come back late." Rahman placed the blanket at the foot of the bed and walked to the door. "He'll come back, he'll come back."

"Rahman," Omar raised his voice slightly. "What's happened?"

Rahman said, "There is a problem between Tok Guru Bahuadin and Pak Zaki."

"What kind of problem? We never heard anything."

"Happened yesterday," Rahman said. "Tok Guru Bahaudin said that Pak Zaki is a trouble maker. Tok Guru quarrelled with

Pak Zaki about it. Now we don't know what is going to happen."

"Where is he now? Tok Guru Bahaudin."

"I don't know. Maybe at the *madrasah*." He left the room.

Sara said, "You knew about this?"

"You heard him." Omar said, "It happened yesterday."

Sara said, "I want to go home."

Omar, arranging a mat and some bedclothes on the floor and changing into *sarong* and vest, said nothing.

She picked another tape at random and played it. "*...the purpose of this talisman is to make you invulnerable. Take a coconut-leaf rib, a betel-leafstalk, or a match-stick, use it to measure the distance between the base of the nose and the upper lip, that is along the groove there, hold your breath and recite* 'Bismillah' *seven times,* 'Fatihah' *once, and* 'Selawat' *once. Then recite this incantation,* 'I take from myself to transform myself'. *Then break off a length of the stick equal to the distance between the base of the nose and the upper lip, and put it on your navel, using a bit of plaster to keep it in place. This talisman will protect you against bullets and cast out all fear in facing any threat from the enemy...*"

Suddenly he said, "I'm going to the *madrasah*." He changed again into casual clothes.

She said, "I'll come with you."

"You stay here."

He stepped out briskly but Bakar stood hesitantly in his path, with a friendly smile. Bakar said, "Not safe to go out."

"I want to look for Tok Guru Bahaudin."

Bakar led him out to the verandah where two others were sitting. One of them tilted his head slightly in recognition of Omar and said, "You've come. That's good. More than thirty people joined this week."

"How many today?"

"A few."

"Where are they?"

Bakar pointed to a chair and waited for Omar to be seated, then he said, "All the information you need will be given to you soon. Be patient."

"Is it true that—"

"Don't listen to Rahman. He's only a boy, he doesn't understand these things. When Tok Guru comes back, everything will be clear."

"Has Tok Guru Bahaudin been expelled?"

"Tomorrow there will be a *ceramah*. He will be there. Pak Zaki will be there. You can hear yourself."

They talked again about the materialism that had invaded the cities. The time for the fight was very near, the time for sweeping away the corrupt legacies of the past, so that a pure society of only believers could be established. We must train, and we must be disciplined. We must be patient and wait for the right time to come out and lead the country.

The chill night air blew in occasional waves across the open verandah in which they sat. They had warmed to their topic and were unaware of the foetid damp that came to rest on their shiny faces and made their loose clothing limp. Their words, unnaturally loud, echoed round the leaf-laden compound and filtered through the open doorway to the room of the secret listener who absorbed their meaning with a sinking heart as she thought: I have made a mistake and I have left it till too late to do anything.

8

Seated among the women and garbed like them in a long loose garment with a cowl, Sara shifted uneasily. Her unfamiliarity at being covered completely except for her face was only a minor discomfort. But was she a betrayer of her faith? True, she couldn't accept that it was necessary to flaunt her belief.

"Look at Papua New Guinea," Panglima once said to her when she tried to say that everyone should be left to practise their own beliefs. "The Christians didn't leave them alone. And what about Sarawak. They were doing the same thing on our *orang asli*. We have to stop them."

He had discovered the power that came from standing up for religious belief during his early life in south Thailand, a period few knew much about. After a quarrel over a creamy-complexioned girl brought down from Chiengmai whom he seduced before the brothel owner could initiate her, he had come to Songkhla by the sea near the border with Malaya where he met and married a Thai girl who was Muslim and he converted to the faith with the name of Saiful.

The Buddhist governor of the province at the time refused his village permission to build a mosque. Saiful was a natural leader in the demonstration which followed. A grenade exploded under a bridge near the police station in Narathiwat.

After ascertaining that it sent a passing patrol jeep out of control into a rubber tree on the side of the road, Saiful went with a following of over one hundred people to the police chief to discuss ways of maintaining peace. Permission for building the mosque followed. He became a member of the Liberation Front which demanded from Thailand independence for the southern province of Patrani and brought his skills in intrigue and quiet menace to a fine pitch.

Sara considered Panglima obtuse because he did not perceive the contradiction between his stopping other people spreading their faith and spreading his own. The colonialists had gone, was the whole business repeating itself? Different groups were scrambling to put their own brands on people. Just like the colonialists, she told Gita later.

The *ceramah* had begun promptly at nine and had been going on for more than half an hour. The speaker inside the crowded mosque was not visible. His voice over the loudspeakers was crystal clear, switching from Arabic quotation to Malay commentary, the words bathing listeners, inside the mosque and seated in groups outside on the wide, sandy ground, like a medicinal oil, refreshing them, making them tremble with slight spasms. Quiet and soothing at first, the voice rose to a declamatory pitch that excited a few women to involuntary cries. Then the voice sank again to commence a new rhythmic cycle.

Everywhere the people were seated in quiet groups on the sandy ground. Except that the atmosphere was subdued, it might have been a country fair or a picnic. A few large angsana trees spread their leafy branches over the entire *halaman*. The men dressed in *baju* and checked *sarongs*, wearing skull caps, sat under the shadiest one, their knees drawn up. The women sat apart, their billowing clothes folded round them, their faces cowled or masked.

The speaker told of people in the past who were traitors to Islamic teaching. In Spain after the fall of Islamic power people were forced by the Inquisition to convert to Christianity. Before the rise of Islamic power what were they, she wondered. Yet when freedom of religion had been proclaimed by the successors to the dictatorship of Franco, many who had retained their Muslim faith secretly over the centuries came out in the open against the many others who now embraced the new ideologies of the *kafirs*, nationalism, liberalism, democracy and secularism.

Gita remembered the Church of England padre, Reverend Buttrose, whose last mission before he came to Kuala Lumpur had been somewhere in Africa. She had been invited with a few other students to dinner at his Kenny Hill house, a typical two-storey colonial dwelling in brick with wooden floors for the upper level. He spoke of the yam meals he had eaten with his flock in Burundi. He offered Gita and her friends one sausage each and a little mashed potato. She laughed. After dinner they sat in the spacious drawing room with its tall Corinthian pillars and large open doorways, and carpet of intricate design, and shaded lampstands, and talked about the decline in values in the modern age. It seemed they were in agreement. It was altogether a pleasant evening she said, as she got up to leave. She wasn't prepared for what came next.

Gita said, "He raised his voice a little and said, 'Before you go, kneel down and declare for Christ.' I stood looking at him and he said, 'Kneel. Just say you are for Christ.'" Sara watched her. "I muttered something to say I couldn't, I think so, but he was urgent, so pressing. I said to him no, but he was looking upwards and his hand was already on my head. Finally—finally I did."

"What?"

"After he had given us dinner what was I to do? I didn't want to embarrass him by refusing."

Sara said, "You mean you knelt."

"What was I to do? He practically forced me down."

"And you—you 'declared for Christ'."

"I don't know. I think he said some words."

"So you are a Christian then?"

Gita giggled. "No lah, how can. I still go to temple to pray." She said reflectively, "Well I don't know, maybe he put a charm on me, how to say?"

The voice stung back into Sara's consciousness. The Christians not only colonised, they waged a battle for the minds. Egypt was the first target, then Turkey: they were influenced into implementing secularism saying, "*Politik suku agama suku.*"

That was *murtad* which means treachery and betrayal of religion. In Turkey, Ataturk too implemented secularism. A Saudi scholar urged him to repent. Religion must rule the world. Set up religion in the face of the earth and rule the world. If we neglect this task we are guilty of betrayal.

"You remember Juliana Mangkil? The small pretty girl with a round face. Third-year student," Gita said.

"Who?"

"The one who was late with her essays. I sent her to you, remember?"

"That one. She disappeared for two weeks."

Gita said, "You know why? She told me she was going to be absent without leave. Why, because the Head wouldn't give her leave. She came to see me in my room. She said she had to go back to Sabah, she wanted to hand in her essay after she got back. I say no, I want a reason. Her face was red, she was going to cry. Finally she said, 'My father needs me. They're trying to make him a Christian.' I said, 'You're a Christian, aren't you?' She said, 'Yes. But that doesn't mean he has to be one.' She was gone before I could say anything. I didn't report her."

If we go to Russia or American we have to follow their road laws. How can religious laws be less powerful than that? It is God who gives government to those He wants and takes away from those He doesn't.

As a crowd the people murmured their assent, Omar with them, and the murmur rose to the foliage of the trees which sheltered them with benevolent guardianship, and ascended to the sky and thence to the moon, the sun and the stars and all that lay beyond.

Between Omar and Sara as they walked out was a space as if they were walking on opposite edges of a ravine.

Omar said, "It's quite natural you should sit with the women."

"Where is it so written?"

"You dare to ask questions like that. You have been brain-washed."

She said, "Tell me one thing. The men can sell their goods anywhere, their stalls are all around the *halaman*. But the women sellers, they're kept at the back, behind the mosque. Not only that. There is an attap fence to hide them. Why? Is it bad to see them selling things?"

They were shuffling out together with the rest of the congregation which spilled out on to the road, bringing the cars to a standstill, as couples and families stopped to exchange greetings and to converse briefly before they moved on, energised by the speaker's assurances of security of their world and how they must deal with the alien. The air was charged with warmth and emotion.

Bakar was waiting for them and led them to the open area on the other side of the road where several open huts stood close together, the plank walls weathered dark brown by rain and sun sloping rakishly, their attap roofs askew. Cars were parked haphazardly in the open space around. Somehow the structures remained erect and people entered and sat on long benches at rickety tables and ordered rice with *korma* or *rendang* or pieces of chicken fried hard and dry. On the table that slanted owing to the slope of the hard earth under their feet, were some stale *kueh* under plastic meshed food covers.

Bakar said quietly, "You must go back home by another way. There may be trouble at the seventh mile. Some people say it's a crazy lawyer from the city who's gathering friends here. Other say it's Tok Guru's people in Jerangau protesting because he has been expelled."

Omar said, "You mean Pak Zaki has won?"

"No lah, don't ask me. It's too confusing, I don't know. Better just eat your *kueh*, drink your coffee and go. Turn at the *mamak* shop there near the electricity sub-station. Quietly walk only, don't stop."

Sara followed Omar on to the road without conscious volition. Beneath her veil and long robes her skin itched. The crowd was thinning; a couple shot past them on a scooter, the woman's full black outfit flapping in the wind like a huge bat's wings.

They turned into the *kampung* lane just after the electricity sub-station. The *mamak* shop was shuttered but that was to be expected when there was a *ceramah*. Sara felt a new desolateness come upon her which the stark light of mid-morning in the coconut grove through which they walked only accentuated. They passed a low brick house with a sprawling compound and several fruit trees. Rambutan skins lay scattered on the sandy ground. From the cemented verandah which sloped owing to erosion, an old man, barebodied, stared at her. The narrow lane was splattered with lumps of buffalo dung.

Other houses along the lane were also shuttered, their compounds deserted. They quickened their steps when they heard a gunshot, Sara clumsily lifting her robe and breaking into an awkward run in the thick-soled shoes which Omar had bought her.

As soon as they got into the house, she shed cowl and robe and put on a loose blouse and tapered slacks. Her cheeks were flushed and her forehead which she had mopped with her handkerchief was beaded again with perspiration. She said, "Can I talk to you?"

He looked at her, unblinking.

She fixed her eyes on the floor near him and said, "I said last night—"

He said, "Better you go in. Shameful for you to stand outside for all to see dressed like that."

"I cannot go on, *abang*. I have to leave."

He glanced outside and said, "Everywhere we go there's trouble."

She said, "Did you hear me? I want to go back. Back. Back."

"It will be okay, you'll see. Just be patient."

"I came because I really wanted to try. But where are we? What are we doing in this house? It's no use, they'll never take us to Jerangau because there's trouble there. *Abang*, can't you see, we've come for nothing."

They did not speak any more. The house was stuffy. Sara walked down the steps of the verandah and stood in the sandy compound. Sunlight shone through the trees. Sunlight burnt the rough asphalt of the lane until it seemed in the distance as if there was a shadowy pool. The *kampung* on the flat land on the other side of the *sawah* was hidden by green vegetation shaded over by a noonday haze.

He shouted from the raised verandah, "I know you've got a man, there must be a man."

She stood still when several gunshots sounded. They came across faintly from the distance sounding like solitary exploding firecrackers on Hari Raya. When one shot sounded nearer she turned and walked into the house and straight into their room.

He followed her. He said, "Do you know where we are? This is the only place that is really our own. Why do you want to go?" She didn't answer. "You did not guard yourself when you were in the States."

"What do you mean?"

"Now you're like a stranger in your own country."

It was no use: he did not understand her. But what he said was true. Less than a year ago, she had been excited after her return from America. There was work to be done, changes to catch up with, problems to resolve.

She said, "What about you. Why are you leaving the city?"

"You don't understand. We will emerge when the time is ripe. This country is ours. We will make it our own."

In the night she awoke to find him straddling her, thrusting the blanket away with his legs like a dog kicking away sand with its hind legs. He gripped her shoulders hard, pushing his face against hers. She lay unresisting, leaving him flailing. In a frenzy he shook her repeatedly as if to arouse passion. She remained motionless though the blood on her lip tasted salty, and her eyes stared observantly at his struggle. When he caught his breath he said, "You can't change just like that." Outside the gunfire had ceased and the stillness of the night flowed in. "Why have you changed? Is there a man?" He slapped her arm.

"Answer me *sundal*. I know there is a man." Still she lay motionless, only staring.

He stood up and said, "When I find him he will be sorry. You—you also will be sorry."

She cried silently in the darkness where she lay. When the night became chilly she longed for drowsiness and sleep, as images crowded: the darkened street with a single spot of light where the hawker beat his *wok* with his ladle and tossed his dish of dry fried *mee hoon* several times, Yun Ming's bedroom window through which a little moonlight seeped in, the wake of the ferry boat on the moonlit river, the dry stubble of harvested fields in Safiah's farm, the television pictures in New York of the May 1969 riots, and Dahlan's bloodshot eyes looking for a way out of the hate that surrounded him at the *dewan*.

She thought: I have wanted to be free and now I am. With that came panic and wakefulness. Outside there was an uncertain light; within, an untidy gloom.

She caught sight of her startled face in the mirror of the dressing table next to the door. She pushed the door open.

From the compound came the sound of loud voices in conversation. Bakar was talking from the elevated verandah with Rahman at the gate. Their voices bounced against the wooden walls of the house and flowed down the passage past her door. Omar, sprawled among the bedclothes, stopped snoring but didn't move.

Bakar turned to her and said, "Trouble. In the old town market area there. Near the shopping centre."

Bakar got it from Rahman who got it from his friend whose uncle ran a petrol kiosk near the Jerangau jetty which was three quarters of a mile from the shipping centre. A motorist who stopped for petrol gave a few details. The area had been cordoned off by some people looking for a group of outsiders from another state hiding in one of the shophouses.

"Tok Guru?" Omar said. He had stepped out of his *sarong*, his upper torso bare.

Bakar shook his head and said, "No. It seems there was a crazy fellow, it's his fault, want to give his *ceramah* to the public in front of a church, huh. Just asking for trouble only."

Sara asked, "Who is he?" But she knew.

"Not our people. From the big city."

Omar said, "Did you know him? Rahman, who is he?"

Rahman said, "I don't know what happened. That was on the road going to Ulu Besut, not in the town. After the trouble started he escaped, his friends helped him."

Omar was pinching his chin with thumb and middle finger to pluck out a hair.

Sara thought: What does it matter? It's the same story of the same madness. If people were alike, there were always some who said some were not, and then bands of people roamed the streets and fought other bands of people. If people were not alike, bands of people roamed the streets and still fought other bands of people too.

She went inside the house and telephoned Gita. An old man's voice answered. "I don't know where she's gone. I'm waiting for her. Every night I sit up and wait for her but she never comes. Who is to look after me? Can you tell her to come back?"

Sara said, "Isn't your housekeeper there?"

The old man's voice said, "She cannot do things like Gita. Yes, she's here. Gita was supposed to come on Friday. She didn't come. Where is she?"

Though he was frail, his clasp was of iron, she thought. Aloud she said, "Uncle, I will help you find her. But can I ask you a big favour? I am now up north, and—"

He broke in. "North! That's it. She said she was going north. How can she do this?"

Gita, too. She rang off, put a few clothes in a plastic bag and said to Omar, "I'm sorry I treated you badly. I think it's best to break. I'm going now."

He was silent.

Outside, Bakar said, "Why are you going? It's dangerous to go alone at this time. Women, especially. You better look out. Wait. I'll ask Rahman to take you to the bus stand."

9

I opened my eyes hearing Sara calling me. She was seated on the floor beside my bed. The scarf covering her hair, knotted in one corner, was askew, she was wringing her hands, her eyes were red with weeping.

"No," she cried. "No, *abah*, no. Why didn't you tell me."

Safiah put a hand on her shoulder to say it was God's will, all that He gives us we must take with gratitude. Sara would not stop. "I should not have gone," she said. She said that many times.

She plucked the scarf from her hair and flung it away, she looked again the sweet tousled child I had loved. Allah forgive me, more than her brothers. It was on my knee that she learned to love numbers. From me she learned to speak Arabic, to modulate the vowels to her voice. The pure, unbroken melody of her voice was her own. When she read the Quran, all the fixtures of the material world faded and the crystal clear tone prevailed over all.

She would have a hard life. I did not think such a thing then, but there were times in the middle of her childish prattle when I looked into her wide eyes and felt a foreboding.

She cried again, "*Abah*, I didn't know."

I said to her, "My dearest child, who is to know what is in men's hearts? Those four men came after dinner. They came up the steps coughing politely, smiling only slightly. Even if you knew, it would have been no use. What can one do in these times? The one in the green robe looked towards the river with a stony face and said nothing. He was the leader. He had taught the others what to say."

I have taught generations of students the Quran, even such at these. My eyes are getting bad now, but I'm sure one of them was that boy Najib, Rashid's son. He spoke fiercely but his eyes wavered. They looked at the wall, the floor, my hands, shifted all the time.

I said, "Safiah, give my child some tea."

Safiah came back with the pink syrup Sara loved as a child and she took a sip of it, then her face became a mask as Safiah told her what they said to me: My teaching was not in accordance with what was laid down. I must change. It seems Bang Kamaludin my brother and his family had been challenged and had admitted they had approved my teaching. I should tell them—the four—everything I knew, they said, so that I could be re-educated to be of service to the community.

Sara said, "What did he do?"

Safiah said, "What was there to do? What to say? He had nothing to tell. That was the trouble. They didn't believe him. They were angry."

Lucky for me, Safiah was there when it happened. She couldn't return to her house after visiting Zainab and her baby because the trouble had started again near the Hindu shrine. I was talking to Sara in a place packed with people. We were talking at the top of our voices and laughing because things weren't worse. I had gone through—what had I gone through? It didn't matter. My legs didn't move, they felt curiously at rest. As if they didn't belong to me. I told Sara don't cry, remember the sweets I used to give you to stop you crying. Mak was angry with you when you did give me a sweet, she said, and that made her shoulders shake. She tried to catch her breath between crying and laughing. My ears were filled with a rushing sound and I was on the side of a gorge and Sara was calling out to me from the other side, calling and laughing and pleading.

I told her Najib stopped to speak to me in private, as the others went down the steps to the *halaman*. I was pleased by this, my teaching was not in vain. He knew the beauty of belief. He saw how orderly it made our lives and how tolerant it is of those others who are not of our faith. He spoke respectfully as to his old *cikgu*. But his eyes were wild. I should have known. They held me in a fixed stare, shifted to the floor momentarily, then came back searchingly to my face. What he said was bitter to take. "Return to the path, *cikgu*," he said. It's not what I've done, but what I've not done, he said. His words struck me like a blow on the chest.

Who is to know what is in men's hearts? The men of all races who kill today in the towns are fathers, brothers, sons, who love their families, who go out in these dark days and unsettled nights in defence of what they believe and come back and boast they took part in operations to pluck 'fruit'. *Jolok manggis*, they cry. Truly, it is only Allah who can forgive them for taking the lives of the innocent. Why did they slice the soft flesh of the infant child snatched from her mother's clasp. Why did they splash buckets on the woman they defiled to revive her. They had wanted her dead. And still they wanted her purity. Then they returned to their homes, their clothes damp with unnatural sweat.

I am not a traitor, I said to Najib. I too have spent hours considering why our history could not have been otherwise. So often have I been filled with hate, Allah forgive me, against those who do not follow our ways. Then I see in the *lorongs* and on the roads young girls of all races holdings hands trustingly as they walked and the hate becomes confined. Allah help me, it will all go away one day.

I tried to tell Najib all about this but my heart was full to bursting on seeing the stony look on his leader's face. My chest and arms were pierced by skewers, my ears sang with a humming sound, and I could not believe the numbness that swept my body away. I see the world's muted colours as if through a thick gauze through my window. I hear Sara's voice as from a distance now. I am in a dark cave surrounded by strange echoes.

How can I tell my beloved child there is nothing to forgive, only love to be given. I understand her grief completely. With my lips I tried to tell her so. I whispered the words and she bent her head closer straining to hear. I shouted with all my might. After some hours I realised my lips and tongue were skewered too, like my friend Vathanam when he carried the *kavadi* from the Sri Mariamman Temple during the last Thaipusam. Sara was sobbing on my chest until Safiah pulled her away. Now she knows that I know. Now she knows that I knew.

There are so many who want to force you to follow the right path. Each one's right path is the only one. I am tired of seeing the folly spread in the name of such right paths. I fear those who seek to come between me and love for all humanity. They are the source of hate and destruction.

It is time for Sara to leave Omar. She should have given him children, Safiah says, then things would have been all right. She offers to bring a *bomoh*.

Through the gauze-like mist I see Sara's fear. Her mouth is framing words I do not hear. I follow the radiance at the end of the tunnel, but turn to look at her again. I couldn't get up in the morning, she said. I couldn't pray. Wear the *tudung* also, I could find no peace. I cannot blame Omar. He is really a good man. He too is searching. I cannot blame anyone but myself.

Poor child, I think she lost her judgement in choosing to go with him to Jerangau. I learnt she went only after she had gone. That is why she is inconsolable. Sara, my beloved child,

I knew from long ago that you would have a hard life and hard choices to make. The fear I had then has not gone. The daring you have been blessed with is given to few. I watch and I pray, I understand why you did not tell me you were going. I understand why you have come back. I will try to understand if you decide to go with that young Chinese.

Whose are the limbs now stretched before me. Why does no one hear my voice? In the days when I took you to the market, you skipped and chattered like a sparrow and you sang as sweetly as a magpie robin. Ah Heng the 'vegetable lady' gave you some *kana*, and Din smiled at you as he carved the meat for our *rendang*. My legs were strong then.

I walked miles during the Japanese Occupation to work at their camp and get their food rations. When the British came back, I walked some more to the office where I worked. After *Merdeka* I looked at my legs and thought: I may grow old but my legs can still be as strong as they are now, how can they not. I have seen a storm advance upon our *kampung* from the hills with ferocious rapidity. Why did I not understand what it really said to me? Life changes swifter than a flash of lightning.

Those legs are no longer mine, the waist, that body. It is too tiring to want them all back. The arguments of those whose view of the world is right, the killing, the desperation of the innocent. I heard Sara say I must live for another twenty years. It is frightening. The lightning flashes more benignly now. It warms me. Sometimes things are so black I don't know where

I am, and I wait for the next radiance. When it comes, I know it will be a thing of great beauty. I will follow it even though I hear Sara calling.

10

A BLIND MAN was playing a cha-cha rhythm on a cheap accordion. One of his two companions played the tambourine, looking sightlessly down the pavement. The other groped at the knobs of a synthesiser, adjusting the rhythm accompaniment to the cha-cha beat. They sat on low stools, knees wide apart behind their instruments. An upturned hat lay on the pavement in front of the accordion player. After a minute they stopped while the rhythm was adjusted; then they resumed with the same tune. They played without emotion.

Saturday morning, and the town centre was beginning to fill uncertainly. On two sides of the huge, dark rectangular concrete shed that had served for decades as the central market, hawkers of fruit, *nasi lemak*, cakes and sundry hot breakfasts Lined their barrows in a row. Water freely from taps and hoses to freshen vegetables or wash plates slimy with the remnants of *kway teow* or *nasi lemak*. Everywhere there was a sticky wetness, on the concrete floor of the market, on the broken asphalt of the roads around it. Cars and motorcyclists revved sedately past as if not knowing what to do with less crowded streets. A bread-seller honked the old-fashioned rubber horn on his 70cc motorcycle. People quickly gathered round the large aluminium container on his pillion and the piles of loaves packed in plastic bags and hanging in cascades on either side. They dispersed furtively with their purchases. Other pedestrians walked cautiously. Some of the shops in the pre-war, two-storey line of buildings on the other side of the narrow street were shuttered, their folding iron grilles locked. The Chinese Medicine Hall was open, and the tyre shop in the corner, and a coffeeshop with 'Rumah Tumpangan Yuen Fatt' above it. A few shops had been smashed open and looted. On the road outside one of the shops, by the drain's edge, were dark red stains now dry, glistening dully in places. Slogans were daubed on the pillars of the five-foot way.

Dahlan peered through the wooden louvres of the Rumah Tumpangan Yuen Fatt and waited for Gita. After a feverish night he had awakened to the sounds of 'My Way' in cha-cha rhythm coming up from the street. His left eye was closed, his lips felt puffy and he couldn't breathe deeply. He got up from the bed with its yellowed bedsheet and gaudy blanket and limped to the dressing table. Gita had left a note. She had gone to see if the car was okay, and she was going to call a doctor. Outside there was a sudden commotion: shouts, the stamp of running feet and a policeman's whistle.

The street became half-empty. A few cars started their engines noisily and drove off fast. People looked expectantly at the streets as if waiting for a sign. Then the normal bustle returned.

Sitting near the wooden window louvres and staring down at the scene below, he thought wearily: I am in real trouble.

He remembered that after his talk in the grounds of the Buddhist temple in the old part of the town, a man came up to him and asked him for a light and the next instant four or five people had set upon him. When he was on the ground they kicked him in the groin and stomped on his face and ribs.

Gita said, "Lucky thing some people from the temple ran out to help. There was a terrible fight. They were throwing bottles at each other. I saw one man running, his face was all covered with blood. The road was fill of broken glass. I did not dare take you to the car. Two of the temple people helped us to hide in a back lane. I don't know how it spread. It seemed like there was fighting everywhere. I saw cars on fire. We crept away mostly in the dark, mostly along back streets. We dashed across roads. Finally, Chew brought us here. Chew is one of the temple people. He said he would help us get away today."

Gita took off her scarf and loosened her hair. She was in a *baju kurung*. She said, "One window is smashed. The radio's gone, and one front tyre is punctured. Otherwise, the car's okay. Let me put this plaster on you." She pulled out a box of band-aids and selected a few strips of plaster. He turned his head obediently to her.

He said, "How do you know the car is okay. You mean the engine."

"I got in and started it. It's fine."

"What about the puncture."

"The guy in the corner shop will do it, but he said we must wait. Looks like all the cars in town have come to him for repairs."

Dahlan said, "We can't stay here long." He said he would be all right. He would try to change the tyre himself.

"You might be recognised."

They decided to ask Chew to do it. Dahlan went back and lay on his bed.

"I never expected such a crowd. You remember when we got here. I simply told one of the temple officials I was going to speak that evening. I think he spread the word. I just intended to give an impromptu talk—my usual protest, nothing else. All of those people who came, they wanted more, you could see that."

Gita said, "You are better known than you thought."

"Did you see the light in their eyes when I was speaking? It had nothing to do with me. And I am not an eloquent speaker. I speak too much like a lawyer. I think that they felt relief that someone was saying the things that they had been thinking all along. That frightened me. It was like bringing it all out, the things that had been suppressed. Nobody with any power seems to have cared for the fears of these people."

She said, "You scared me the longer you spoke."

"Why?"

"You did become more eloquent."

There was a knock on the door. Gita unlocked it and Chew walked in. He was a spry figure with greying hair neatly parted at one side and a pleasant smile with false teeth. He was a teacher in a Chinese school. He said things were bad in the old quarter of the town where the temple was. About seventy people had died, many more were injured.

Why had he risked his life to come, Gita asked.

Chew spread out his hands and said, "You are our guests. We must take care of you."

He looked at Dahlan's face, shaking his head as he did so. He said, "They wanted to hurt you. I have brought you some herbs. Soak them in hot water and bandage onto your wounds. Sure you will get better quickly."

When told of the puncture, he said he would change the tyre and bring the car. "Don't mind if I ask uh," he said to Gita, "Have you converted already? If not, better you don't show yourselves too much."

Gita told him where it was parked and gave him the keys.

After he left, she got some hot water from the coffeeshop below and bandaged the herbs on to Dahlan's cheek with her scarf. She said, "Better this than nothing."

He left feverish and did not speak. He dozed for a while, his breathing sounding like a light snore.

He woke suddenly and said, "You said I scared you when I spoke."

She said, "Sleep some more. We can talk in the car."

"I've slept enough."

The blind men's three-piece band had ceased to play. The morning sounds around the market place had given way to the intermittent noise of horns, motorcycles revving and diesel-engined lorries moving on first gear. The sun's heat rebounded from the street's broken asphalt dazzling the eyes of the pedestrians who bowed their heads and hurried on. A faint stench of rotting vegetables hung in the air.

He persisted, "What did you mean?"

She said, "You were really impressive—in an eerie way. Your voice came over on the mike very clearly. After the first few minutes your pronunciation was perfect, your words came over in a caressing manner. I have never heard you speak like this before. Your voice was quiet at the start, then it worked to a high pitch so much so that some people applauded you and clapped spontaneously.

"Then you would start again at a conversational level on a fresh cycle. You switched from Malay to English and back smoothly and naturally. You spoke about religious persecution through the ages and religious intolerance and forced conversions. You spoke of what the Spaniards did in Mexico to the Aztecs, and in Peru to the Incas, what the Moors did to the Spaniards, what the Portugese did in Brazil, the Belgians in the Congo, the Kampucheans under Pol Pot to their own kind in Cambodia. You called it an act of perfection in inhumanity the way the Spaniards converted virtually an entire Southeast

Asian nation to Christianity and totally obliterated their culture, taking away even their race-name and replacing it with a derivation from the name of a Spanish king.

"And then you asked why we hadn't learnt the lessons of history well. We took the lessons so far as it suited us, and for the rest, continued to perpetrate the same cruelties against our fellows. Finally you said, we should never accept that we are fated to be victims. If we did, it would be our fault. We cannot blame race, background, the government, history or the position of the stars for our condition, however bad it may be. We should not wait until the final calamity was upon us. We must rise up and attack every encroachment on our freedom."

He stared at the ceiling and said nothing for a long time. A great exhausted sadness filled him, a sense of being lost in the stream of history. Sadness for Gita, for Yun Ming, for Sara, even for Chew who seemed more rooted than all, sadness at the fragility of their world. He thought: I've made a terrible mistake. He did not know where to hide.

There was a knock. She said, "That must be Chew."

At the door were two men Gita had never seen before. She tried to close the door again but they stepped coolly inside.

One had a v-shaped receding hairline, a drooping moustache and a goatee beard on a square face. He wore dark glasses and a Hawaiian shirt that hung over his trousers. He stood motionless and looked past Gita to Dahlan lying on the bed.

The other was a barrel-chested younger man wearing a tee-shirt and flowered Bermuda shorts.

The man with dark glasses walked to where Dahlan lay and said, "Are you going back today?"

Dahlan pushed himself up and said, "Who are you?"

The man said, "You're going back to the city?"

"Yes. Who are you?"

The man said, "Okay, we'll give you a lift. Pack your things."

"I don't need a lift. I've got my own car."

The younger man in the tee-shirt stepped forward. "Maybe you don't understand. We're taking you back. Now get up."

Dahlan said, "But—my car—"

The man in the Hawaiian shirt said, "Uh-huh. We've taken care of your friend Chew. He doesn't want to repair your car anymore."

Gita said, "We don't need a lift from you."

The man in the Hawaiian shirt pulled up a chair and sat down close to Dahlan. "If she doesn't shut up, and if you don't get up now, I'll make your face look even worse."

Dahlan got up gingerly. Gita went to his side, saying, "He can't move now. Let him rest. Who are you anyway?"

The man said, "Tell your girlfriend—"

"My wife."

"Tell your wife not to interfere, or both will be hurt. Got all your things?"

Gita said, "Wait, where are you taking him? Why?" But she recoiled when the man in the tee-shirt showed her a knife.

The two men pushed her away easily, took hold of Dahlan on either side, and walked him out, the wooden floor and stairs of the old two-storey lodging house creaking under their tread. Gita waited for them to emerge on to the street below, but realised after a few minutes that they were walking on the five-foot way running underneath the room along the front of the shophouses. She ran down the stairs shouting, "Dahlan!" and pushed past the marble-topped tables of the coffeeshop where people sat. She looked up and down the length of the five-foot way, peering above and round the wayside sellers of trinkets, but Dahlan and the men had disappeared.

11

It was restful here in the old quarter of Malacca, to stay in his room on the ground floor of his father's house with the shutters open and look at the unmown grass and the lean brown creepers that dangled loose from the giant *tembusu* tree. When Yun Ming stared at the dense green heart of the tree he recaptured fleetingly the foolishness he felt at coming back. His booking of a telephone call from Bangkok to Sara in the early hours of the previous morning; the operator trying the two number he gave her and getting no response; his sitting in dazed immobility on the bed; the call again from the sympathetic operator who had somehow sought out and connected him to Sara's father house. How did she get it? He felt he and the operator were the only voices echoing across the empty vastness of that night. A woman who answered at the other end of the line asked why he called at such an early hour. Nothing he said made her understand. He first felt foolish when impulsively he packed and left Bangkok—"for urgent personal reason", he told the ambassador.

The aeroplane left an hour late but after twenty minutes the stewardesses were snapping shut their food counter doors;

there was a bomb alert and the plane returned to Bangkok, taxiing to a floodlit remote corner of the airfield where they fidgeted for a while. They got out and stood on the tarmac while the luggage was unloaded and individually identified with each passenger. Then they went back to a departure lounge and there they sat or lolled for six hours. They became fleetingly a community asking tentative questions and getting vague replies, hiding their anxiety behind gripes about lack of sleep and food. A voluble Malaysian began talking about how in another flight a pistol-packing aide of a Minister refused to be searched and still was allowed on: he swaggered about the aircraft but the pilot did not turn back. The Malaysian started another story about a bomb which exploded in a suitcase on the conveyor belt, but nobody wanted to hear him.

Bangkok was outside; here they were in a cocoon. The men in their griping and later in their dulled expectancy began to resemble the city's smirking, foreign men, white, black, yellow and brown. The stewardesses lost the look of tailored elegance their Paris-designed uniforms gave them and began to look and talk more like the young country girls with wistful eyes and the painted, older girls in short skirts in the bars of the city.

•   •   •

Penang in the morning in streaming sunshine. He had chewed with gusto into the bacon which he would not get to eat for a long time again, and picked desultorily at the mushroom omelette in the airline breakfast tray, too disoriented to mind the voluble Malaysian who moved to the empty seat beside him. The Malaysian asked him the usual question: what he did, how much he earned, why he was going back. "I just want to see some people. Business," the Malaysian confided, as if in return. He ran a bed-and-breakfast place in North London, he said. On two fingers of each hand he wore large rings with stones bulging out. He turned the rings round on his fingers as he spoke. "I'll stay a week, then I go back. How about you?" Yun Ming said he didn't know.

"All this trouble. So unnecessary, man. It's still a beautiful place," the Malaysian continued. "I really like it. A land of opportunity." He saw Yun Ming's questioning look and said, gesturing with his hands for emphasis, "It is still better. Better than England." He lowered his voice. "Road blocks everywhere. I have to go extra twenty kilometres just to get my friend's house. From Sungei Way can't go straight, you know. Try and see. Why build a highway, ask them. Highway cannot use, only for military trucks. Which military also I don't know. Formerly we were all together, remember, in school? Now see if you can find a Malay and Chinese, just friends. Not for money, you know, just friends. Where. Tell me where."

After the landing in Kuala Lumpur, Yun Ming allowed himself to be led by his companion into the immigration hall, his shirt sticking on his back, his eyes registering the faded tourist poster, the huddled groups on the other side of the glass partition peering through to catch sight of an expected familiar face. The Malaysian handed Yun Ming his card. It read "HAVERFORD LODGE. Manager: Tony Z. K. Pang. 15 rooms. Central heating. TV. Shower. From £15 including full English breakfast."

Pang said, "If you need anything in London, contact me. Accommodation, I'll give you a special rate. Actually the lodge is only a sideline. I deal in property; you want to buy? So many people I have helped to get property. Flats, houses. Some of them Ministers. Top people."

Yun Ming could not help asking whether any of the Ministers were going to be clients this time. No, but there was a lieutenant-colonel who was interested in a flat in Hampstead.

Under the shadowless lights of the customs hall, Yun Ming looked a crumpled figure, face shiny, indistinguishable from the tee-shirted males waiting for passengers to come out. Disappointment showed in the face of Pang who, with abrupt coolness, gave a slight nod and made his way to a waiting car.

Emerging from the customs hall, Yun Ming was surprised to see his elder brother, Chris, unsmiling, waiting for him.

Chris took his bag and led the way out. He said, "I asked the Ministry for your flight details."

But how did he know Yun Ming was coming at all?

They drove through the stricken city, the mid-morning sun exposing without shadow derelict or burnt vehicles, some overturned, lying by the roadside, bonnets propped up. Ahead of them was a roadblock manned by soldiers and some civilians, and queue of cars. Chris swerved into the side lane branching off the highway and was slowed down by soldiers directing traffic. The traffic lights were not working.

An announcement was being repeatedly played over a loud-speaker fixed on a metal arm jutting away from the traffic lights. "...the situation is under control. My intention is to preserve the country against lawlessness and disorder. The terrorists are trying to make a comeback under cover of political and religious parties. Do not listen to rumours. Give your fullest cooperation to the security forces in the maintenance of peace in the country."

Chris said, "Listen to him. Hundreds of people dead all over the country, and he hasn't got anything to say but that." It started two days ago, he told Yun Ming. Bomb explosions more or less simultaneously in five major towns, near temples, churches and mosques. Chaotic fighting between different groups followed, but with rumours of police and army defections, it was clear that the central government was no longer in control. The country was now divided into three zones, Eastern, Northern and Southern each claiming to be separately run.

Chris was wearing dark glasses. His Hawaiian shirt rippled in the breeze as he drove. He said, "I couldn't have come at a worse time. If not for Father I would have scooted back. They brought him home from the hospital. Not enough nurses to give him attention. All on emergency duty. Fortunately the radiation treatment seems to have had a good effect. I came back three days ago when I got the message. We were wondering why you weren't back sooner."

Yun Ming's mind was racing. He lied. "I was upcountry from Bangkok on a trade visit."

They drove past the old shophouses in Brickfields and got back again on the highway going south; a vast rubbish dump spread out on the left, then green hills; the other side of the road had been scraped dean of vegetation; wet laterite soil stretched flat away for a mile; *kongsi* huts and large signboards advertising a new housing estate stood in the barren expanse.

Chris said, "Who was that big shot you came with? Seemed to know all the Customs fellows."

Yun Ming said, "He lives in England. Wants to sell London flats here. What's it like in Brisbane?"

Both hands on the steering wheel, Chris turned to look through his dark glasses momentarily at his brother. He said, "Good. You should come too." Yun Ming couldn't see his eyes through the black lenses. The head was prematurely bald with a few greying hairs curling from the centre. The facial skin brown and slightly pockmarked, the hunched shoulders more solid-looking than Yun Ming remembered. He might have been a lifeguard.

Chris said, "There, it's simply open. Do what you want. Go where you like. Not this kind—" He stopped. "What are they trying to do here? I mean, are you happy? Can you be happy with all this going on?" He nodded his head a few times as if in answer to his own question and his shoulders too moved: I told you so you wouldn't be.

Chris took off. He and Karen and the children bought a house within one week after they got to Brisbane. That was three years ago. Lovely. Wall-to-wall carpeting. All it needed was a washing machine and an oven. And some odds and ends. They took one look at the government school near their place and Karen said no way she was going to let Cindy and Billy get mixed up with those rough children, and put them in private schools. Two thousand a month. Well, it's what they wanted, they were ready to pay. They met some fifteen Malaysian families within a short space of time. The whole range. From fifteen years in Australia to one year. Chris told them be frank, don't spare us, we're here anyhow. And do you know what? Not one said they had any regrets.

"What about all those racial incidents?"

"Aw, come on, man, sure there's some racial feeling. Sometimes an Asian gets bashed up, but don't believe everything you read. Much of it is exaggerated. You know they're such friendly people."

"We're friendly, too."

Chris said again, "Yeh, like now. Come on, why do you stay when all this is going on? All right, you're getting good money, but how good is that? Why do you want to stay, now that you and Phyllis are not together? You won't have a chance here, you think you'll ever get to the top? I hear there's a Malay chick you've taken a fancy to. Okay, go ahead, play the field, but don't get caught. Add a few notches to your gun, sure. And then come, there's nothing here for us."

Yun Ming said, "Chris, cut it out. You don't have to talk like that."

Chris said, "All right, all right. Let's get down to business. You have to wait till he's gone. That's what we're here for, right?"

"I've come to see my father."

"Isn't it true? I mean, of course I'm concerned about the old man, but we all want to know what we're getting, right?"

They were driving through flat *padi* land, divided by bunds into neat rectangles from which the *sawah* bent in dry brown sheaves. In one rectangle further away from the road, two buffaloes lounged in the mud; a crow stood on the nape of one. Then they were passing through an older rubber estate where overhanging branches, linked over the road in a continuous arch, casting a gloom over them after the bright daylight of the open road.

Yun Ming said, "Do you go surfing?"

"What?"

"Surfing. In Brisbane."

"Oh. Yeh. There's some really good stretches of beach outside Brisbane. Some weekends we just dump our things into the jeep and head for a quiet spot. The kids love it. Or we go camping. It's a good life."

Just a lifeguard. Fair dinkum.

He lay down to uneasy sleep. Images jerked across his mind: the Thai stewardess, the acrid smell of octane and the noise of aircraft engines in the airport, the haunted eyes and postured hands of the people peering through the glass partition of the immigration hall like figures in a dance of death, the loudspeakers at the traffic lights, and the noonday drive across the country with a brother he had never liked. He awoke to darkness, then stumbled to the window and opened it out wide. A great two-storey house; ochre-washed, ornately designed walls; the unmown lawn turning brown under the sun's heat; the bright flame of the forest tree with fewer blooms than he remembered; and the massive, darkly mottled trunk of the *tembusu* outside his room.

When he arrived, the house had been almost completely shuttered, only the front door was ajar. Ah Peng came out and took his bag. His father was resting upstairs, she said. He was well, sometimes he had a little pain, and sometimes when he couldn't stand it, he groaned. The medicine was all right, a nurse came every morning. He slept a very long time. In the morning, he came downstairs and walked about. He had just had lunch: some *bubur*—it was better not to disturb him. The darkened room, their talk in whisper, irritated Yun Ming.

The instability outside had penetrated the house. His father, he knew, would not yield, but he saw that he consciously, and Ah Peng unconsciously, were preparing him for it. He did not want to be at the mercy of events, but the closeness of the atmosphere was overpowering; it filled him with a feeling of apprehension. Ah Peng caught her breath exaggeratedly when he went to a window and opened it wide; reluctantly she opened the rest. A portrait of his father and, on the opposite wall, a boar's head, hung in shadow.

So when he awakened in the evening to his darkened room, it was to a panic that he had failed to perceive the real danger of the course he had embarked upon; that it was a mistake; and that he was not going to turn back. He went down the passage past other rooms, stopping at one with a door left ajar. He peered at the dark-brown mother-of-pearl display cupboards and the round marble-topped table with squarish-designed chairs neatly arranged round it. They gave the room the spacious look of a museum except that his father's work-table lay at the far corner with it piles of papers arranged with unusual neatness. He tried to tell himself it did not look like a room already vacated.

He went to the front of the house and was surprised afresh by the bright daylight that streamed in through the windows and the fully-opened front door. The amber light of the late evening sun fell on the dark leather upholstered settee and on a glass cabinet filled with small, silver shields and silver cups. His father was sitting in an armchair looking at the driveway, his thinning hair neatly parted, his face shiny, as if after a wash, and expressionless.

Yun Ming said, "Father."

His father said, "So soon you've come back. So how is Bangkok?"

"Father, all right."

They were silent for a while, listening to the hum of the traffic in the distance.

His father said, referring to Chris, "Yun Tat has gone to Damansara, I don't know what for."

"I think to look up his old friends."

His father stared without blinking at the driveway. He said, "They want to know what is it like live in Australia. Have you brought any property in Australia?"

"No."

"There was a good chance. Residential property in Melbourne. I didn't want it. I wanted to call you."

For his father, nothing had changed. He didn't have to like the people he lived among or did business with. He just made the best of it, pressing for an advantage, a money opportunity when he could. He had come to Kuala Lumpur from Sitiawan at the age of seventeen and worked as a lorry driver transporting timber from deep in the forest to shanty towns that sprang up as rows of single-line plank huts with brown corrugated zinc roofs at intervals along the rough, winding road going to Kuantan. He became close to a local *kapitan*, visited the *penghulu's* son. When he got a forest concession for logging timber in the Permatang Forest Reserve, he opened a sawmill in Temerloh, which looked the most promising of the shanty towns. For a man who made his fortune as a timber merchant, things would go on. There was always a lode of richness in the earth waiting to be picked. It was a matter of knowing the right people. If some fell in battles with rival groups, it was your bad luck only if you didn't have friends in the rival group. Old man Chung married the daughter of a tin miner and had friends where it mattered. He was not interested in the troubles except if they affected the movement of his lorries.

After his father had been helped back upstairs, Yun Ming drove in the lengthening evening to Seremban and picked Sara up at the Rest House.

12

Iт sтоод оn a hill overlooking a lake and its black-and-white
wooden structure wore an air of shabby gentility from pre-
war times. On the opposite side of the lake amidst new laid
garden paths rose the large-domed mosque, also new and
white, asserting an alternative aesthetic. Its flood-lit reflection
quivered in the lake and flung a gloomy pall back over the old
Rest House.

He stepped tentatively into the lounge and picked her out.
She wore a pair of light-blue pants and a white shirt hung over
it. He picked up a newspaper from a magazine and rustled it
as he read intently. Then he walked out. A few minutes later
she joined him in his car.

He began to race along the old road over which he had
driven so many times that he had ceased to notice its sharp
bends and the stretches where it narrowed unexpectedly.
Then they were in a queue of cars moving slowly towards a
checkpoint. She combed her hair with swift motions, parting it
differently, curling it, fluffing it. She ran a lipstick over her lips,
wetting them with her tongue as she did so, and dabbed her
cheeks with powder from a compact. Then she snapped it shut.

He looked at her and said, "Hullo, do I know you?"

She said, "I'm your Chinese girlfriend", and they laughed.

A loudspeaker was playing patriotic songs. A soldier with an M-16 looked at his papers. Another stared at her.

Excitement grew on him, amounting to numbness, a feeling of spinning in a vacuum, and he looked attentively at the objects his headlights jerkily caught in momentary focus as they moved on the pitch-dark road; a lace-fringed *kampung* house window half-hidden by the foliage, the gleam of a cat's eyes as it dashed into and out of his path, a shadowy cyclist picked out by the rear reflectors of his bicycle, a *sarong*-clad farmer with a cloth draped around his bare shoulders, on a sharp bend an old provision shop below road level lit by a yellow kerosene lantern, three youths lounging on a plank bench. They were like points of reference holding him from complete surrender to the heady rush of air and the drone of his car engine as they descended into the plain that extended towards the sea.

In the hotel room, once they had shut the door, they clung to each other, still and wordless for several minutes. She marvelled at the violence of his passion which blanked out thoughts of the world outside, and her fear of people who spied. She fought back with an energy that surprised her, discovering previously unfelt sensuality. The slight shame she had experienced earlier, when the bent figure of a bony Chinese clerk handed them a key mutely when Yun Ming spoke to him in Cantonese, was swept away by relief that he was now part of her loneliness.

She thought: What will happen to us?

The question sobered her, became an accusation. She opened her eyes, hardly aware of the desolation in which they were, aware only of the windowless cubicle in which they lay, the old air-conditioning unit that vibrated loudly, and the bewilderment that attached itself to her like pain. The image of her father lying without power to move his limbs made her close her eyes. This morning he had been better: his face did not twitch. When the telephone rang, there was even a twinkle in his eyes as of old. Yun Ming spoke haltingly, elated that he had got her at last. Where was he, in Bangkok or—? Oh. Yes. Yes. Yes.

She tried to frame in words the feelings that made her dizzy. Phrases ran through her head as she drove up the road to the Rest House. Casting a glance sideways at the handsome white mosque across the lake, she was startled as she thought: I will not go back. The words penetrated her sense of security. She knew then with fearful relief that her way was desolate.

They awoke from a deep slumber and he held her face in his hands for a long time.

He said, "I called and called. Never got you. Always Safiah. You were gone, she said, but she wouldn't say where. Was it Jerangau? I thought you were leaving later."

"It's a village about a hundred and twenty kilometres from Segamat. In the old days people used to travel up and down by boat. Now they use the new road the government built."

"At last, I just took a plane and came."

"But you didn't know where I was."

Yun Ming said, "All I know is that I had some notion I was going to look for you."

She looked at him and said, more to herself, "Was that why I came back?"

"What?"

"You won't laugh if I tell you?"

"What? All right. I won't laugh."

"I was thinking maybe that's why I came back. Because somehow I knew you were coming back."

He laughed.

Then he saw her eyes become moist and he cradled her head against his shoulder.

"Sara."

She did not respond.

He said, "You know the real reason why I came back and why you came back?"

She felt warm in his embrace but still she remained silent.

He said, "Because we're both mad."

She laughed and rubbed her eyes with the back of her hand.

She said, "It was difficult getting back."

"What did Omar say?"

She said, "It's not Omar, you don't understand. You don't want to believe what you see. I think that's the difference between a man and a woman. A man loves a woman but he is also interested in other things and can easily turn away. I have a problem. I love you like hell and that's all that matters. Omar couldn't stop me from leaving him."

He felt confused, and had not words to reply. At last he said, "I meant it was dangerous for you to travel alone through such a large black area."

"Black areas, white areas, it really didn't make such difference then. I don't think it makes much difference now. Some places when I was coming back in the bus were just Malay places, some places Chinese places, and some places, well, they were Malay-Chinese-Indian places. Everywhere there were soldiers. What soldiers. I mean they were just men carrying guns. Every few miles they stopped the bus. Our driver would bargain with them. Then he came in and said, '*Lima Ringgit*' or whatever, and each of us had to pay. At some places it was more. If we didn't have any more money, we gave a pen, a watch, a bracelet and so on. I was tired, and hungry. We stopped at Gemas to get some food but the whole place was a mess. Streets littered with rubbish, one row of shops burnt down. Uniformed men everywhere, waving their guns at us to get off the streets. We didn't get much chance to buy any food. I only wanted to go home, see my father, and then find you, and ask you, is this what the search for identity is about. You work for Panglima, you know the big shots. Tell me, what are you all doing about this mess?"

She watched as he got up and poured out a glass of water from the coloured Hong Kong-made flask with a dirty cork top that stood on a side table. He wiped her wet cheeks with his fingers. The furrows in his face deepened, making him look old, as he held the glass while she drank.

He said, "I thought I was doing a lot. I'm not sure anymore."

She said, "Why?"

"I don't know."

"But Panglima? I think they rely on you a good deal."

He said, "I really tried to believe the things he wants me to believe. I want myself to believe. I want to believe them. But I can't. For them, I'm just a token, that's what I've realised. They'll readily give up the things I believe in, which they say they believe in, if it suits them. And kick me out. Panglima, too. Panglima especially. So what the hell am I doing working for them? Who am I working for? What am I working for?"

She said, "The young men who came to the house and told my father he's a traitor—they had no problem with belief. They left him paralysed from the neck down from a stroke. My father a traitor. And he ran that school for forty years. One of them was a former student of his."

"Sara."

"Yes?"

"Come back with me to Bangkok."

"But my father."

"Yeah, I know. Mine too. So?"

She said, "What I want to know is, what did those young men want my father to do?"

"Be like them, what else?" He put on a voice: "I'm very different from you, can you see that? See how I dress, this is the only way to dress. See how I pray and love God, this is the only way to so such holy things. You have nothing, you must follow me, do as I do. Live as I do."

They sped along the road leading to the coast until they joined a queue of cars behind a slow-moving oil tanker. Here the road wound round low hills planted with rubber trees and across short stretches of *sawah*. From somewhere behind the thick banks of cloud that covered the sky entirely, the afternoon sun cast a pallid light over the gaping hillsides of a new development scheme which they now passed.

They found another boarding house in Remis, and stayed in their room until evening, closeted from the world outside. He persuaded the old woman who refilled their flask of water to buy them food. She handed him fried noodles and fizzy drinks, her sunken cheeks creasing in a friendly smile that exposed shiny false teeth as she asked him confidentially, "Is she Chinese?" After they had eaten he pushed her roughly to the bed and she suppressed a cry even as she held him.

Later he told her about himself. His family had been in Sitiawan for three generations. When his mother died, his father removed him and his brother, Chris, from Chinese school and put them in an English school in Ipoh. His father said, "You will never forget your Chinese. Learn English now. It is very important." He and the schoolmates he met in later years from time to time—a director of a mining company, a couple of doctors and lawyers, with one Datuk and one Tan Sri thrown in—by common inclination looked back fondly to the time when they were hardly aware of race. Arshad—later the Datuk—went to the mosque on Fridays, but was otherwise one of the gang who played rugger and cricket and badminton and were made prefects by Mr. Sanderson who turned out to be the last English headmaster the school was to have.

But there was an occasion when talking to Datuk Arshad at the end of a party at the latter's house some years later, he felt a fleeting uneasiness when anecdotes about their school days cropped up again. Datuk Arshad who now had a neatly trimmed beard and moustache in the Middle Eastern manner was not communicative when Kumar asked him about the law then being proposed about *hukum hudud*. Was it intended to be applied to all? Yun Ming suddenly found himself speaking tentatively, withholding sentiments he would have freely expressed in the past, alarmed that he did withhold them, furtively closing over his alarm as well as his artificiality.

Panglima, whom he met at a *muhibah* party after May 13th consoled him, "At least you had a conscience." But he said, superciliously, "You think you related to each other in the 'good old days?' That is the final colonial legacy—Happy Subjects. You were brainwashed to think so."

Yun Ming said, "Just look at it from the human point of view."

"What were you? Schoolboys on the English model. Did you read poems of Rupert Brooke, Henry Newbolt—*Vitaï Lampada* and so on? Don't look surprised. I've done some reading too. I know the trap."

"We could crack jokes about race. We can't do that now."

"You were fellow subjects. Everything was planned and done for you. Now? Now you have to really understand."

Understand what?

Understand us.

(What about understanding me?)

For such a realisation to come upon him after May 13th— that was the stunning part; that it took so long. He felt embarrassingly stirred by a patriotic impulse that was sniggered at. He wanted to work for the brotherhood of all. Some said that was patronising. Towards whom? He asked, but he knew. He knew also there was more than a grain of truth in the criticism. It had all become a matter of language. He was usually honest in his perceptions, but he felt justified in suppressing those that didn't help in the realisation of his new goal. He resolutely sought a complete re-orientation: he found that that involved disregarding some obvious facts. It was a little like not telling the whole truth. He found an argument to justify this as well. He thought: I may be wrong but if disregarding a fact will make a bridge, I will disregard it. Maybe, just maybe, that was path to truth.

But Sara made him see the artificiality that coloured the patriotic impulse both in himself and in the new post-May 13th ambience. It was an exhilaration not to have to choose one's words before speaking. Nearly everyone else did choose, that was the trouble. They pretended not to see that they had reduced language to token gestures, a process in which only a few were speakers but the vast majority became only listeners who used truncated structures and novel usages that engendered a certain fellowship but arrested thought.

He grasped Sara's naked form tightly to him and she awoke. He said, "Will you come to my father's house?"

She said, sleepily, "You know I had a lovely dream. You and I were in a wood, there was a well near our house. Our neighbour came to invite us to dinner in his house. You were in your working clothes but you did not want to dress up to go across. I begged you but you wouldn't. At last you said if the neighbour gave you a sweet you would change."

"Did he?"

"I don't know. You woke me."

He kissed her and said, "Let's go. I want you to meet my father."

13

Sara gazed at the shining mirror of the sea as they drove along the coast road. Clouds, orange-flecked, cast a glow over the atmosphere. Behind them the sky had darkened and a group of starlings rose and wheeled in crescent formation before darting behind a promontory.

In the bustling crowd of the one-day fair at the seaside, where they stopped, they were nearly anonymous. Dresses, jeans, coloured scarves, batik shirts, balloons, rubber toys hung closely together from stall to stall: they had to duck frequently to walk along the narrow passageways along which people brushed past each other. She paused at a costume jewellery stall and fingered a necklace of Sarawak beads thoughtfully. Yun Ming bought it for her and put it round her neck.

He said, "These are worn by the Dayak maidens in Sarawak."

She touched the beads round her neck gently.

He added, in a whisper, "Bare-breasted", and laughed at the apprehension in her flushed face as she turned this way and that to see if anyone had heard. "You're too much."

As he swung the car inland the brilliant beads glistened in the evening sun.

Immediately afterwards, the gloomy tops of rubber trees became a webbed canopy under which they sped. Sara became aware of parting folds of darkness. The car was silent and hung in space. *Sooner or later they will catch us.* Why was it important? Why was it not important? Death would wipe out all rules, mock all mores, end all revered genuflections before the unknown. She only wanted her father's blessing but he was on his death-bed and would not speak. She wanted to tell him why she came back from Jerangau, why she left Omar. None of it would make sense, he wouldn't understand, what with the country gone mad, but she would tell him nevertheless. Now one had to be prepared to negotiate with conflicting guards of three ill-defined zones. Human beings were mutilating each other. Hate, dread, suspicion and loneliness had entered into every house. She and Yun Ming—her father's eyes were fixed on her and tears gradually welled in them. She tore her scarf from her head and flung it to the ground weeping, "I shouldn't have left you, oh, why did I go?"

Yun Ming said, "Did you hear that?"

She opened her eyes.

He said, "I didn't mean to wake you."

"It's all right."

He said, "The radio." A choral group was singing. The tune though melodious, had become, by repetition, a bore. "Just now in the news: an underground group has caught Dahlan.

The group is prepared to release him in exchange for some of their own now in prison."

She said, "They will kill him before that."

She told him how Dahlan and Gita came to where they had been; he had given one of his *ceramah*; the commotion; his capture.

He said, "I don't know what to do any more. He's a stubborn fellow."

"He does things in the wrong way, but he makes me feel guilty."

They were driving down a lane with thick, tall hedges on either side when the lights of Yun Ming's house appeared some thirty metres ahead, yellowing the darkness. Yun Ming stopped in surprise. The aroma of broiling *satay* filled the air; thin, blue smoke cast a light veil over the people who sat at makeshift tables laid out in the garden. They were like spirits from an underworld. Above the noise of general conversation there were occasional bursts of laughter.

Chris came out to meet them with a mug of beer in one hand and bowed with exaggerated deference to Sara whom Yun Ming introduced as his colleague to whom he was giving a lift. Chris said, turning to a guest he was talking to at the time. "Do you know Arasu? We've known each other from primary school." He launched into a school anecdote about the two of them and their form master—something about stolen rambutans. Arasu and Chris laughed heartily.

Somebody said, "Is it you?"

It was Gita wearing a veil draped round her head and shoulders and a *baju kurung* which glistened under the neon lights of the porch. Her eyes, reddened as though from fear and anxiety; and her dark lashes, betrayed restless energy.

She pulled Sara into a corner and wrung her hands. She said, "I know you're going to be surprised. Dahlan and I are married."

Sara stared at her.

Gita said, "It just happened. I'll tell you about it another time. But—but—they've taken him. It was after his speech— you heard? There was trouble there. He was beaten up. Then two men came and took him away, and I don't know where he is, and I don't know what to do."

Sara said, "Who were these men?"

"I don't know. I think Panglima knows though he pretends not to. It was no use calling you, you were in Jerangau. I did not know you were back. Then I called Yun Ming to help me get through to Panglima. His brother answered and asked me to come down. So here I am. When did you come back?"

Sara said, "I'm back for good. I have left Omar."

At some tables, guests had finished eating and sat conversing over piles of used plates, forks and glasses of partly-drunk syrup.

Yun Ming said to Chris, "Why are you doing this when father is upstairs ill?"

Chris said, "Not to worry, he's asleep. A nurse is with him.

Besides I couldn't meet all my friends with all the disturbances going on. Have a beer. By the way, is she your girlfriend? Be careful, uh, you may lose more than your skin. First you chose English, at least this time you could pick Chinese. How come you didn't?"

Yun Ming said, "You could have shown a little respect for father's feelings."

"Always a worrier. I am showing respect, I don't expect him to die. There's no problem now, is there? He's still asleep."

Yun Ming went up to Gita who was standing with Sara in a *satay* line which was not moving. Gita told him about Dahlan.

He nodded. "I heard."

She said, "Please can you do anything?"

He said to Gita, "With so many rival groups it's hard to say who's got him. Sure Panglima knows some of them, but to them he's an official."

Gita said, "There must be something he can do. Maybe just even talk to them, send a message. Anything. I know he doesn't like Dahlan, but I'm afraid something may happen. Please Yun Ming, tell me what to do."

"I'll talk to him."

A short lady in a *sari* with a bare, bulging waist started talking excitedly to Gita.

Yun Ming said to Sara, "You haven't seen our house. Come in and take a look."

She followed him past the grille door at the threshold.

He said, "I'm sorry I didn't know Chris had arranged all this."

They stepped into a lounge area crowded with leather upholstered furniture, and the glass panelled wooden cabinets revealing pennants, small silver shields, and silver cups neatly lined on the shelves.

She asked, "Yours or Chris's?"

He said, "My father's. Here, look at this one. Nineteen twenty-eight. Hundred metres hurdles. This one—high jump."

She wondered what it must have been like in colonial days to run in the school sports and be handed your prizes probably by the wife of some white education official.

"How's your father?" She suddenly felt it would be interesting to talk to him.

Yun Ming said, "He's asleep upstairs. He's been in and out of hospital. He went in again last week. We brought him back. His mind's wandering."

Sara simply looked at him.

He said, "Cancer. It's too far gone. It's got to the bone."

She still said nothing.

"We brought him back only the day before yesterday." Yun Ming spoke in a manner-of-fact tone of voice. He pointed to a large stuffed head of a boar mounted high on the wall. "See that? He shot it. He loved hunting."

She looked at the large colour portrait of his father hung high on the wall near the staircase. The face was expressionless as if nothing could dismay its owner.

The hunter saw again the solid wire-haired beast. Its cigar-shaped body was pointed at him, it snorted and then it charged. He took aim coolly. He heard neither the blast of his shotgun nor the screech of the wounded animal as it jerked violently and rolled over. He only knew as he pulled the trigger that it was just right.

The days of vigour were gone. There was the old man upstairs lying in bed, his mind wandering. Could he make anything of the hubbub of conversation below, and the bursts of raucous laughter, and the rifle fire across the country as life ebbed away from his body? Sara looked up again at the boar's head. It seemed to stare her out of countenance.

She said, "Take me to see him, anyway." She climbed the staircase with Yun Ming.

•   •   •

They drove in the darkness with only the car's parking lights on. Slowly at first, until Yun Ming's eyes became accustomed to the dark, then at a moderate speed.

He said, "We can reach your father's place at about six."

There was little traffic at this hour. He took a long detour into a *kampung* to avoid one military road block, bumping on the sandy village road, twisting between houses on stilts, backing away from dead ends, and looking for new ways out he revved the car to a high whine and it jerked forward again.

Could the journey on the other side be the same as this one?

Mostly unguided, strenuous, without illumination, in hostile territory. Could there be nothing? She clutched at Yun Ming's arm, moving closer to him.

She said, "Do you think your father saw me?"

He didn't reply.

She said, "I want my father to meet you. I think he will like you."

She said again, "All those people. They have seen us together."

He said, "They're going to see us together a lot more."

He put his arm around her and said, "Get some rest, close your eyes."

She awoke with a start to see Yun Ming reversing the car swiftly, and turning back.

He said, "Another road block. Too many soldiers, too many road blocks. What's happening? We'll go back to Remis and stay there till morning."

At the old lodging house no one answered their knocks on the door. At last, the old woman with shiny false teeth appeared, grumbling in Cantonese. She shone a torchlight in their faces and said, "*Tada, tada*", several times. "*Ada orang, yo. Jaga baik-baik.*"

Yun Ming turned the car round and they headed out of the town again.

He said, "Full house there. Where next?"

She said, "I don't think that's what she meant. She was warning us."

He turned into a laterite road through a rubber plantation.

She said, "Where are we going?"

"We'll stay here a couple of hours and then try our luck by another route."

He stopped the car where the road curved away from a high bank, and switched off the lights. They sat still listening to the night sounds rush in on them. The sound of water from a running stream somewhere down below quietly gurgling, soothed her. Here there were no houses, only the worn out bumpy laterite road, the rubber trees well spaced out, and hilly ground with rough undergrowth arid shorter trees in the background. This area was a haunt of Yun Ming's boyhood. Together with schoolmates he had cycled this way on a Saturday to splash under the cold waters of the stream cascading over large smooth granite rocks which bulged like the backs of elephants down to a green pool below. On one side the spreading branches of a *tembusu* tree wove a canopy over the pool. Behind lay the forest and the paths they had not explored during those stolen hours, stopping where the undergrowth rose thick against their young bodies, leaves and branches brushing roughly across their skin, raising welts. The dark green mass of foliage that lay beyond was something they would explore one day. On this side was the path along which they had come, then their secret path, now a widened dusty laterite road along the bank of the river. The clearing of the undergrowth had brought an unwonted harsh light to the area.

The road was now used by lorries carrying sand dug from the river-bed further up for housing projects on the outskirts of Dusun Lama.

The whine of a lorry engine in the distance awakened her. It became louder. Above it she heard voices talking in Cantonese and broken Malay.

She said, "They're coming this way."

They sat still and listened. The noise of the engine and the rattle of the lorry's bodywork as it bumped over the potholed road loudly filled the night air; the headlights jerked crazily, catching their car briefly, then flashing away up and down and receding along the bank upriver. Among the voices, Yun Ming thought he heard one hooting with derisive laughter.

She said, "I had such a nice dream."

"What."

"It was of my father. He was dressed in Malay baju and sarong. He wore a kopiah and he carried—I think it was a briefcase. He came to see us."

He said, "Us. You mean you and me?" She said, "Yes."

"Where?"

"Uh—here. I'm not sure."

"You mean he saw both of us?"

She said, "Yes. He was so nice, just like when he used to teach me to sing when I was a child. And he said, he spoke to me, and he was smiling and he said 'Look after each other'. Only that."

He said, "What did he say?"

"'Look after each other.' Then he said, 'I can't stay now. I have to go.' And he went. Ming, wasn't that lovely?"

She thought he was coughing but his shoulders were shaking.

She said, "You're crying because you're happy?"

He held her tightly and said, "We must go and see him as soon as it is light."

She said, "I wish I could call him now."

They lay back and the night surrounded them once again. Yun Ming shifted uneasily, seeking sleep which didn't come to him for a long time. In her drowsiness, pictures passed through her mind: the driver of the bus walking down the aisle saying "*Lima Ringgit*", the wrinkled face of the old woman with the unnaturally shiny false teeth, the soldier with an M-16 who tried to peer through her flimsy Chinese makeup, the branches of the tall rubber trees which closed over them as they drove, the *satay* smoke in Yun Ming's house, and his father staring vacantly at her, except that his hand moved slightly in response when she took it in her hands to her lips. She thought: Father said my life would be hard; I do not want to be alone anymore. With that panic came.

Outside hatred and fear pressed upon them. Carnage had flung into the air twisted threads of steel. Hate clouded the remnant stars. An unnatural atmosphere stifled the breath. She was wakeful and mourned the loss of the verdant green which had guided her life and was now obscured by prejudice and mistrust which trampled on everything she found worthwhile. She had been startled by long-forgotten feelings of resentment and bitterness seeing the casual wealth in Yun Ming's father's house. The mounted boar's head was symbol of grating alienness that would never vanish.

She trembled and clutched at him tightly.

14

For some days after her father's funeral, Sara remained in their house in Sayong. She had no clear idea what she was going to do next. She listened dry-eyed to Safiah who greeted her on her return.

"We tried to contact you and Omar," Safiah said. "But the phones were not working, soldiers were ever where, roadblocks. Ah Lek, you remember him, Ah Lek? Bringing us vegetables? He doesn't come so often now. Panglima said don't wait, don't torture the dead. So we went ahead and buried him before sunset.

"On the morning we found him dead, he lay with a smile on his face, the kind of smile he has only for you. He looks at nobody else like that, I think he must have been seeing you at that moment, *ala*, don't cry, don't, no, don't all right, all right. I'll tell you later. You want me to tell you some more or not? When I brought him coffee that day like I did every day he was already gone, may Allah bless his soul. So we covered him and I called you. And when I realised it was no use, I called Panglima. And he and all the others bathed the body and applied the fragrances with cotton wool. Then they wrapped him up in six metres of cloth which I bought from the *towkay* in Kuala Kangsar. We looked after him well. You know in these times, we didn't expect many people to come—but there were so many people. Most of them he taught when they were small. They know you and Omar had gone to the new community. And so hard to travel. So many people came because they loved him, he was a good man. The *Imam* came and the prayers were said, and at last we buried him before *maghrib*. Panglima didn't want me to go to the burial ground but I did. I did it for you and in your name. I didn't cry, although my heart was heavy; I was there for you and we did everything and may peace be upon his soul.

"And you, what about you? You don't have to tell me, *'dik*. I know. This kind of news everyone knows, it spreads fast you know, *macam api dalam sekam*. Don't worry. If he loves you, he will join us. I heard they arrested you. Both of you? And let you go? You escaped? *Ala, 'dik*—don't stand there in the verandah."

She drew Sara into the darkened dinning room at the back of which was a blackened fireplace. They sat at the old dining table covered with a floral-patterned vinyl sheet and Sara found it a relief to let the words stumble out.

• • •

"Najib was among the people who took us. I don't know where they came from, eight or nine of them. I didn't see Najib then, it was dark. They were banging on our car with their torchlights, shouting at us to open the door. Yun Ming tried to start up the engine and back away. But someone pulled the car door open and dragged him out. They beat him badly. How did they come to be there, so many miles into a rubber estate and secondary jungle, if they hadn't been following us all along. Maybe they were the people on the lorry which passed us an hour before. They were punching Yun Ming and spitting on him. When I told him not to, they turned on me calling me the usual names, prostitute, and so on. One of them called Komaran dressed in army fatigues embraced me, touched my breast. Then I noticed Najib. He had been standing in the background, an M-16 slung over his shoulder. He shouted to Komaran to stop. When he came forward he looked at me without speaking. He did not show any recognition. The stony look on his face and his stubbly beard made him look menacing. He had a handkerchief tied like a headband over his forehead. Najib was the one who told my father, his old teacher, to return to the true path.

"They took us to a clearing in the jungle a few miles further in where a community lived. I realised they were a banned group and Najib was a member. On the second night, he told me to wait a couple of hours. We were going to be stoned for *zina*, he said. They were only waiting for their leader to confirm it. Who was their leader, I asked, but he shook his head. I asked Najib about Dahlan. He said in a soft voice, out of hearing of the others, that they got him too. He said,

'I don't know where he is. Maybe he's still alive because they want to find out why he has acted as he has. He may be at the centre. That is upriver.'

"It was he with his shifty eyes and wavering look who, while guarding me, prepared me for escape—and Yun Ming too! What a thing, *'kak*. Najib did that."

·   ·   ·

I don't know when my father gave up. I think he had been giving up for a long time, only I didn't notice, until I came back from the States.

Our house used to be filled with the bustle of people coming and going. The *ulama* and his friends came in the evening and sat in the verandah talking and watching the *sampans* ferry people to and from the opposite bank. Sometimes their voices were loud. There was also children's chanting of their lessons and so many visitors, the headmaster, Safiah and her family, and many others. It was all so happy. Now the house was quieter, people tiptoed in and out. My father was withdrawn. He spoke to me less. I didn't mind at that time, in fact I hardly noticed. I was wondering how to tell Omar that we couldn't go on.

It was enough to come back to Sayong and see my father. I could go down to the river bank and imagine a world where I could be myself without fear. Sheltered by the drooping branches of the angsana tree, surrounded by the quiet whispers of its leaves, and sitting alone by the running stream, I forgot the prying eyes and looks and the snide remarks.

•   •   •

For a long time I have been lonely. I became aware of my loneliness when I realised I could no longer live with Omar. That was in the States. In so many ways we were an ideal pair, people said, blessed with good looks, intelligence and a little money. Poor Omar, he is not to blame. But when we lived together I saw a banality that was crushing. He couldn't understand when I told him I wanted to just go. He said, "I know. You miss home, and your father. We'll go home soon." When I went to bed that night I was so cold.

The loneliness has become worse since they arrested Yun Ming and me. Now he's gone, will we dare see each other again?

There has been no sun for several weeks now. The burning of houses, and the growing piles of rubbish from unswept streets, the dense black fumes of bunting rubber from wrecked cars have created an inverted dome of haze under which we stifle slowly. The daylight has a pallor which makes morning and evening the same.

After a week of confinement to a small room I could no longer tolerate the ogling of Komaran. My contempt for him had no effect: his square balding head framed at the window, he looked at me with a fixed stare. I was depressed by the haze outside, and by the loneliness, and by the waiting. I decide to take my case to the very top, to my *Penaung*, and ask him to help me.

The guards were in a flurry but they could not refuse. I heard Komaran shouting and once he even lurched at me. Najib told him shut up. At last my audience was arranged. Just as I was going out I remembered I had no gift to give my *Penaung*. Would he understand why I brought him nothing?

I remember nothing after drinking the cup of soup they brought me. There was a feeling of spinning round in the darkness. I was walking on a frozen lake in a wooded area with Yun Ming, both of us in thick warm jackets, my hand tucked in the crook of his arm for warmth. They are doing something to me, I said, laughing. He held my hand tighter as we moved unsteadily on the ice with its thin layer of snow.

I was in a vehicle crunching over a gravel driveway. The box in which I was swung high, as if I was being transported to the sky by a mechanical sky-jack; then it swung sideways wide and long, and up again. Two men in cassocks marched me along a corridor and up a flight of stairs. I entered a spacious chamber filled with maroon velvet upholstery, two hanging chandeliers lit with small golden bulbs, and standing shaded lamps, throwing patches of yellow in the corners. The floor was covered with deep pale blue carpeting. The guards disappeared.

At the far end the entire wall curved in a wide arc, the upper half in glass offering a magnificent view of the burning environs far down below. On the left were three large high-backed seats like judge's seats, overlaid with metal which glistened from the lights of the chandeliers.

My *Penaung* walked in without looking at me, accompanied by two persons. All wore shoulder-length wigs. My *Penaung* went up to his chair and sat erect, hands resting on the arms of the chair. His companions sat on either side of him mutely. His curly grey hair was neatly brushed, his features flashy but smoothly cut. He wore a shining white shirt with a yellow bow tie. A flowered handkerchief hung out of his breast-pocket and he wore a red hibiscus in his buttonhole.

When I stepped forward to greet him, he raised his hand. Looking back fearfully I saw a chair placed in the middle of this chamber, fully six metres from him. I put my palms together at my forehead in a gesture of *sembah*. He looked at me for a few seconds and motioned to me to sit down. He spoke in a neutral voice but how could I tell him frankly about my fears, my anxieties, from this great distance. I mumbled an apology for not bringing any gift, but he looked as if he did not hear me. It was time to tell him why I came.

I said, "I cannot stand the loneliness down there among the fires, in the haze. Why are they staring at me? If I stare back they make fish mouths and loud sucking noises. At night the haze sinks lower, coming through the windows with a deadly pallor. I do not want to join them. Tell them to let me go. Let me have the freedom to live my own life in my own way. I won't be any trouble, you'll see."

My *Penaung* gave me a piercing look and leaned back in his chair.

"I am so lonely down there. At least tell them to let him go. I know you are a good person, you won't let us suffer."

They looked at each other. My *Penaung's* gold watch glinted when he moved his hand as he spoke. His curly hair combed backward from a thinning forehead, his slightly flushed cheeks, and his starched white shirt with a winged collar, gave him the world-weary look of an epicure. He said, "We must look at this matter objectively."

He sounded so reasonable I began to feel relieved. I did not detect the menace. Later I realised it was the manner of one who chose to pander to narrowness. So long had he maintained the facade of wise indifference to the appeals that were made, his supporters let him go anywhere, do anything without question.

He said, "We don't want to be rude to you, even though we are judges. But you must ask yourself: have you been fair to us? Has your conduct been satisfactory?"

The bewigged person on his right was a large, yellow-faced man with a curved nose. He jerked his chin upward often like a nervous tic. It was as if his collar was too tight. He said, "You have made us very unhappy. You never consulted us in anything you did."

The third man said mildly, "You have stubbornly done things in your own way. You have chosen not to listen to advice.

You have not followed our fundamental rules. Now when you are in trouble you come to us and ask us to help you."

My *Penaung* said, "Do you deny you have done these things you are accused of doing?"

The yellow-faced man said, jerking his chin, "You have asked to see us in private. You would have brought us gifts if you could have. You really came here to ask us to ignore the rules which you have broken."

My *Penaung* said, "You know this is the highest level to which you can come. You want our help. Very well. Help us to help you. Do you deny what you have done?"

"If I deny it, what about—"

"Leave him out of this. Think of yourself now. We know you are afraid. We know you are sorry."

"If you deny it, maybe we can help you. But if you don't, how can we?"

My *Penaung's* voice retained its careful neutral enunciation. I tried to understand they were not telling me to repent for what I had done nor that I should beg for mercy. They were telling me I should lie.

I felt tears in my eyes. "You don't understand. I know you mean to help me. But the haze and the fires have brought me near to death this time. Please don't be angry. I just want to live out in the open with nothing to hide."

I was desperately unhappy they did not understand me. Maybe they did not really listen to me. They have never lived in the haze, nor amidst the fires, up here in this rarefied hall of deathly grandeur, meting out decisions that suited the generals' or their own lusts, blind to true green beauty.

My *Penaung* said, "We don't want to scold you or punish you. In fact we have been quite restrained although the charges against you are serious. In due course, all will be forgotten. But you must help the process. Leave the past aside, break away from him for good, give up the idea of becoming a martyr. Prove that you are worthy of our consideration."

I could not listen to him anymore, I was so disappointed with the outcome. I had come for answers but a lecture was what I got, all about what I should have done. I know now their heats were hollow.

So I had used up my last chance first. I had come to the highest tribunal and only found three old men mouthing banalities. There was no point waiting any longer. The fires down below that burned our hearts, the haze that choked our breath, had burned and choked the quick in these men. Their hollow voices uttering untruths in pompous tones, their use of process to justify deceit, confirmed that I was at their mercy. Once again I was swung, wide and long in the box; it swooped down until I was on the deserted, debris-filled streets.

•   •   •

Does the consciousness go out like a light too. When the brain is dead is one dead? Perhaps father's consciousness simply receded to another level and he spoke to me from there. His consciousness is my consciousness. His from the 'spirit' world somewhere to mine in a dream. Consciousness receding infinitely till it became as distant as a quasar. Maybe that is what death is. If so one never dies.

The house was always quiet in those days. So long as I was there he lay prostrate and unmoving. Now I know he heard me, he knew, and left at last only when I was far from him.

I got up in the night in my room and stared out at Komaran still looking in, not seeing him, because I was wondering about death, knowing that no one would tell me because no one knew.

I have made enemies without knowing it. We have met in the work place or in the library and we smiled and talked to each other. One day one came up to my door and refused to come in. His dark face was flushed, his eyes mottled red. I had done nothing to him. Maybe tried to help sometimes, but he told me I had stopped him growing. I had prevented him from earning the praise that was his due. I realised that if I denied it, he would become even worse. So I let the people listen to his wild utterings.

Another was white with a barrel for a stomach, and the vilest tongue I ever knew. We worked together for years as friends until I asked him one day not to destroy a mutual friend with his tongue. He became my enemy after that. He asked me to a celebration lunch and pilloried me before the guests. It was like the stabbing of Caeser.

But these were not my enemies. These were people who were insecure, and lashed out at rivals who might displace them, or out of gratuitous hate which they nurtured.

Somewhere there was one enemy I had to track down. I did not know who he was, perhaps he was someone I spoke to often or saw everyday. He knew my movements, he kept a dossier on me. He knew about Yun Ming from the beginning, I was convinced. But I didn't know who he was. If I visited a friend in the evening I knew he would be there. Why was I chosen for this persecution? Was there some mysterious political, religious or financial plot, too complex for anyone to understand?

My life lost its familiar guideposts before I left the university. I had suspicions that I was accused of many things. My superiors ignored my greetings when I passed them—a sure sign that they had received reports about me. What could I say? I knew that before long I would be arrested. It would be at night, without violence, just a request that I should answer for my life.

What they might—would—do to me did not matter but I feared what they might do to Yun Ming. He had been close to them and they would make an example of him. With no hope left in the highest circles, I fell back at last on my guardian, my adviser, Panglima. He was after all from my *kampung* and knew my father and our family well. I was in such a desperate state that I was obliged to ask him for help. His attempts to be familiar warned me that he was not all together to be trusted. But I had no one else to turn to. When I said this to Najib he stared at me without any expression. Suddenly he said, "Tonight I will leave the door of your room and your friend's open. He is here too. When you hear me call to Komaran, get out and run."

Why did Najib help us? Though he did not look into my eyes again, he was again the boy my father taught. His face looked so sad. He wants to believe with his friends and he also wants to believe as my father taught him. He doesn't know why they are not the same. Komaran was my guard and he kept staring at me through the window. He would walk about a little, then he would stop and fix his eyes on me. I went to the darkest corner of the room and turned my back to him. About an hour before the call for morning prayer, I heard Najib call out to Komaran, who grunted and left.

I slipped out of my room and let Yun Ming out. I took hold of his hand and we ran into the undergrowth that encircled the camp in which we were held. We didn't care how the branches whipped us, we had no breath left and still we ran. Then I stepped into a hollow and fell down hard, spraining my ankle. Yun Ming half carried me, and we rested every few hundred metres, panting, listening to the forest sounds of whirring insects, the occasional flutter of wings, and the rustle of branches under sudden gusts of wind. When we got to the road about an hour later, rain had begun to fall in spurts from the dark clouds overhead. I hid in the drain alongside the road while Yun Ming ran to get his car. It was about a kilometre away. I felt so alone lying in the soggy grass, looking up at a sky that had been obliterated, waiting for him to return.

He drove up without lights, not fast, revving quietly, switching his engine off and coasting when he could. When he reached me, he got out of the car and said, "It's better if we go back separately."

"How?" I asked.

"You take the car, you must see your father, go now."

"What about you?"

"I'll get a ride. Go now, don't argue."

I said, "I don't want to go. I'm afraid I won't see you again."

"Sara, if you want, I'll become—"

When I heard him say that I burst out crying and he held and comforted me. "I'll call you when I get back and we'll make plans. If the worst comes to the worst we can go to the Eastern Zone."

I drove the car and I came and it's too late, 'kak, Allah forgive me, I didn't see *abah* before he died.

Sara walked out into the garden and listened to the faint sound of the stream that bubbled below. She did see her father. After he died. When did he die? If he died moments before Safiah found him lying cold and motionless, was that the time of his death? Maybe all that meant was that his heart stopped beating, his blood stopped flowing at that time. But the consciousness? There were deeper boundaries through which it must recede. It did not go out like a light, it did not die at the same time. It just went elsewhere. The last time she saw her father, his lips moved and she read what he told her "I saw a great shining light through which I went very fast, it was so beautiful, I was so far away. Then you came and dragged me back over a dusty, sandy road. Why didn't you let me go?"

This time she was not there to drag him back. But he, on going, did reach out to her. He did tell her—her and Yun Ming—"Look after each other." She looked again into the flowers on the hedge and strained her eyes seeking to penetrate the infinite folds of receding crimson. She sat on a bench and wept letting the sound of the wind on the trees, and of falling branches in the *dusun* drown her racking gasps, and she did not know whether it was for her father, or for herself, or for herself and Yun Ming that she wept.

15

Gita put her ear to Dahlan's swollen lips to catch his mumbled whisper. "...why are you doing this to me, I asked Hsiao, and he only said I would not get out alive. Only when my *Penaung's* helper came, only then I returned to my body and felt the pain. Men were holding me down on the cement floor. It wasn't necessary, I couldn't move much after what they did to me. Hsiao stood holding a stone grinder above my face. Every time I didn't answer who was behind me he dropped it. My nose was broken after he dropped it on my face. When he dropped the grinder again I moved my head. It fell on the side of my face. After the third time I could not open my mouth, my jaw could not move, I couldn't hear well. After that I learnt not to move at all. How many times more they did it I don't know.

"Suddenly I slipped out and watched them from the ceiling. I could see what they were doing to my body but there was no pain now. Another man, Ranatunga, took a pipe, you know a piece of plumbing, about thirty centimetres long, and forced it into my anus. He pushed it deep—so deep—I was shouting, screaming. Then he put a length of barbed wire through the pipe. At last he pulled the pipe out leaving the barbed wire inside me. From above I watched myself scream and scream while he slowly pulled the barbed wire out. I floated through the walls of the room and rose above the trees into the haze-ridden night sky. I landed on the street of Besut where I had given my last public talk. The shophouses were gutted and urchins were searching among the debris, for what I don't know. I remember striding down Jalan Tembeling with people cheering behind me. They said I said things they wanted to say but dared not. When I reached the site of my last talk I saw the bodies of people stacked neatly like piles of firewood and I fell to the ground weeping at what I had done. 'Everything is worthless, nothing is worth striving for,' I shouted. In an instant I was back in my body and I bled in a heap unattended in a silent empty room. I cried and asked to see my *Penaung* and they couldn't refuse me.

"When my *Penaung's* helpers carried me, there was no part of me they could touch without me feeling the pain. I had never seen my *Penaung* before, I think I never will again. His name is Lahab. I was placed on the floor and he and his two associates sat in very high chairs.

"He said, 'We know you want to be a martyr like those in the twelfth and thirteenth centuries. We are sorry you fell into the hands of an outlawed group. But the pain you feel is little compared to the pain and suffering you have caused us all.'

"'Each day after they were done with me I was flung into a

little room,' I replied. 'Its pitch darkness obliterated perception totally, why didn't you save me then? I had no body, I slipped in and out of consciousness and often I thought I was at the start of the tunnel of darkness the dying entered. Why do you say I brought you pain and suffering? I only wanted to stand up and be counted.'

"Vanar, one of Lahab's associates, said, 'So you stood on the steps of a church and a temple to criticise us. Like those priests who stood in front of a cathedral in Saigon in the Seventies and read out a protest. Have you forgotten? They were taken away, we let you go on.' His dark, leathery face shone with perspiration. 'Do you realise that?'

"Tseto, my *Penaung's* third companion, now spoke. His skin was yellow as if from jaundice, his nose was curved, and he jerked his chin upwards and sideways frequently in sudden movements. He said, 'And now you want us to intervene.'

"I cried, 'I can't stand the pain any more.'

"He said, 'Do you want us to tell them to stop?'

"I said, 'I can bear their pain. But not the pain and suffering my words have caused. Help me!'

"Vanar said, 'Do you promise to live by our words?'

"I think I was slobbering before them. I said, 'I have lived all my life by words. I have seen men make them do anything they wanted. That is the evil I have fought.'

"'Evil is part of life and ineradicable,' Tseto said, jerking his chin several times. 'Remember Candide. After he was driven from his castle, enslaved, flogged and broiled on a spit, he said, "Everything is for the best in the physical and moral world." That is what we want to tell you.'

"I said, 'I do not accept your words. You even read your words wrongly. I will fight.'

"My *Penaung* said, 'Fight to the death as of old—if you're prepared to face the consequences. But this is not the thirteenth or fourteenth century.'

"I said, 'It is.'

"'You won't last. You will be forgotten utterly.'

"'There will be others.'

"My *Penaung* said to me impatiently, 'And there will be others on the other side too. Always. You are thinking of al-Andalusia, you are thinking of it in the wrong way. It was glory won and glory lost. Don't forget, Christians fought Arabs, Arabs fought Arabs, Christians fought Christians.'

"I said, 'Out of all these convulsions came the beauties of Toledo, Seville, Granada, Cordoba. Jewish, Christian and Arab scholars and theologians translated and studied each other's works in great centres of learning. The great mosques and libraries of Cordoba, the music of Seville, the works of writers like Ibn Abd Rabbihi, of thinkers like Ibn Al-Khatib, Al-Khaldun emerged from the free flowering of cultures, beliefs and the pursuit of knowledge.'

"My *Penaung* frowned. 'You are a foolish idealist. It was not a free flowering. It was conquest and re-conquest, and though it lasted eight hundred years it ended in the Inquisition. You are on a childish quest. You want to stop the world at Toledo. Do you understand? The end after eight hundred years for both victor and vanquished was absorption, assimilation or exodus.'

"'Who absorbed whom?'

"'That is a mystery of life.'

"'If I am wrong, why then did you consent to see me?'

"And so my best chance ended. I was now at the mercy of Ranatunga, Hsiao and all their vile associates. I didn't know who their leader was until one morning, very early, Hsiao dragged me out, I couldn't walk by myself, and he threw several buckets of cold water on me. He brought me to a counter which was closed except for one panel. I could only speak by bending forward and inclining my head. Hsiao vanished. Inside, several hooded figures sat at tables arranged in rows. Stacked high on the tables and on the floor were files. A figure came up and took my personal details and my fingerprints. Then I stepped into a room, and there behind a large table sat Panglima. He asked me was I surprised, I said no. He asked me if I knew all along, I said no, but I had a feeling.

"He said, 'I said I would get you.'

"I said, 'Yes.'

"'Now I have.'

"'Yes.'

"Panglima's back-combed, thinning grey hair, his slit eyes, and the mouth that widened in a humourless smile, floated separately, triumphantly, before my gaze, like fading after images. He said, 'You have humiliated us by your actions. People like you must be wiped off the face of the earth. You have been guilty of betrayal and treachery. You have been so brave, you must also be brave to die.'

"I said, 'It was you who denied Fatimah Neelambigai a holy burial. The shame you brought us is something you must answer for. Your time for suffering will also come.'

"This time his mouth was a thin line, and his eyebrows arched. He said again, 'You won't be there.'

"I said, 'There will be others.'

"'There's no Minister to help you anymore. Even your *Penaung* won't know what happened to you.'

"I said, 'He will know one day.'

"'You won't be there.'

"'Never mind. There will be others.'

"Everything is quiet now and I watch them from the ceiling. There is little more they can do to my body which flops like a rag doll's when they try to kick it to life. Gita, why are you here. I am tired of those who only play with words and rules. Let us go somewhere else like the Arabs who fled from al-Andalusia to Tunisia and Egypt when the Inquisition started. Exodus, my *Penaung* said. So be it. Let us live our lives in peace in Eldorado, let me dig the garden, and let me plant all the lovely flowers of the world. Gita?"

16

WHEN PANGLIMA LEARNED that Sara had called, he was stirred in the same way he had been when he seduced Niramon the fresh-faced, creamy-complexioned young girl from Chiengmai. Before the brothel owner could initiate Niramon, Panglima had crushed the reluctance out of her and taught her to minister to him exactly as he wished. Unlike others he had enjoyed, he only had to land his fist hard on her lips once, her gums bled and she was pliant or responsive thereafter. She learned to sense what he wanted from the degree of pain he inflicted.

No one would have guessed, from his basilisk gaze and the dangerous quiet of his voice, his humble origins in a derelict corner of Rangoon near the banks of the river whose muddy waters absorbed the jetsam of the city as it flowed into the Bay of Bengal. In this quarter the refuse remained unswept, the shutters of the old two-storey shophouses hung from broken hinges and the last few rickshawmen came back late at night to stretch out in the dark recesses of the five-foot way and suck deeply into opium pipes.

He did not really know his father, and did not know how the old man came to have a knife in his throat one morning, floating serenely, bloated stomach up, the knife occasionally changing his direction as it caught in the tall, thick, brown reeds near the edge of the Irrawaddy. The Karen woman who adopted him said it was the result of a quarrel over opium which his father sold to the rickshaw-pullers. The Karen woman was his father's common-law wife; perhaps his father was Karen too. He spoke the language fluently enough, and regularly sold clothes and trinkets to the Karen upcountry and came back with opium. All that suddenly became the past.

When a few days after the burial, his adopted mother asked him to sell the cakes which she placed neatly on a tray made of palm leaves to be carried on his head, he ran away, and was found some years later working in a brothel in Had Yaai in south Thailand under the name of Ram Prachart. Some of the girls in the brothel believed he was a Thai of Indian descent, others that he was of mixed. Cambodian and French ancestry. All agreed he had Malay features.

When the Japanese landed in Kota Bahru in 1941, he crossed the border into Malaya at Sungei Golok with his wife, and won their attention by reporting the black-market activities of certain Chinese merchants to the local Japanese commander. Shortly after, their heads were among a row of twelve arranged in a row on Jambatan Ismail Petra in Kuala Krai.

After the invaders moved rapidly down the peninsula he went as far as Kuala Kangsar where he was put in charge of distributing rations of rice, flour and sugar. Nobody asked where he came from. Rumour had it that he was from Acheh in North Sumatra, a story he encouraged. Other rumours referred to his sexual prowess. By this time, he had acquired a fluent command of the Kedah dialect and become a feared and respected figure among the *kampung* folk whose influence he successfully peddled in post-independence politics.

Sara reminded Panglima of Niramon in many ways. She returned from America wearing jeans oftener than not and he could not keep his gaze from the shape of her back nor from the way her shirt hung sometimes loosely out. She was voluptuous without knowing it. Her brown eyes with dark curling lashes and her golden complexion maddened him. He wanted to save her for the good life.

Panglima spoke to her father about the way young girls dressed now. He said, "They must be controlled."

Her father said that in some countries women and girls went uncovered but they were still very moral.

Panglima said, "In some countries they are caned. They are much better after that." He spoke about *hukum hudud* as the way to ensure morality but her father was not listening.

When Sara got her job in the university, he assured her father that he would look after her, since Omar was away so often. Once when she stayed for a weekend in his house, he addressed his wife in her presence and spoke of the necessity of punishment to encourage modest attire.

Sara said, "Both men and women?"

He said, "Women are the great tempters."

Sara switched on the television while his wife cleared the dishes. Sara came less frequently then. He flew to Phuket and consoled himself with two teenage girls whom he left weeping after a violent night.

On the night of the concert when he came to pick Sara up, he drove with her into an unlit lane and wordlessly held her in a vice. She was startled to find his square face with its slit eyes nosing her with blind power. She squirmed with pain but sank into his grasp more completely. At last she fell limp and he glared at her in surprise. He shook her but she did not respond; the desire left him suddenly. He started his car and drove to his house where his wife was waiting. They did not speak a word. At the *dewan* as they walked up the steps he said to her in an almost neutral voice, "One day you'll be sorry." When told she had left with Yun Ming before the concert was over he said to his wife, "She has no shame to go with a stranger."

Now she was in his power. He let her call a few times before he took up the receiver.

She said, "Can Panglima help? Dahlan and Yun Ming are caught. Can I come and see you?"

He said, "It's not good for you to be involved in their problems. Better you stay quiet and don't meddle. Anyway, what's Dahlan to you, why do you worry? He's created so much trouble. Sooner or later he was going to get it."

"Panglima, please help. They have been caught by a group near the Zone border. Those people will do anything. But worst is they may send them to the Northern Zone. If that happens they may even be killed. Najib is with them, I saw him. Panglima please do something quickly. If you send a message at least they may be warned."

He said, "You were caught by Najib's group? I heard you both were caught. Is that true?"

"What?"

"You and Yun Ming. It's shameful. So soon after your father's death, how could you do this? You have brought shame on all of us."

She said, "Panglima, I know you are my Guardian. I ask your forgiveness. I will explain to you, I must see you, I will explain to you everything. But please help them first of all. I'll give you all the details now."

"I'm not free now. I have a meeting with the Minister. We have to go to Lipis. You better come and tell me everything."

"When will you get back? Oh, it's urgent, they could be killed."

He said, "You made a big mistake joining with them. You have been too loose in your behaviour. Better you don't have anything more to do with them in future. Then I can help you."

She said, "Yes, yes, I will do anything you say. But please help, I know you can help. Yun Ming was your loyal worker."

"After what he has done, if they don't get him, I'll get him. I'll see that he's sacked, he'll never get a job with us again."

She said, "If you don't help him now he will be sent to the Northern Zone. Maybe even tomorrow. We'll never see them again."

"Why do you care about him? Do you know you're in big trouble for being with him."

"Panglima, I ask your forgiveness. I am truly sorry. I hope you will understand when I explain everything to you. Please help me."

He said, "I told you I'm not free now. My meeting with the Minister I don't know when I'll finish. Then tomorrow morning early we're going to Lipis."

"Can I see you after your meeting?"

"After my meeting I'm going to my house in Durian Badak. I told you I don't know when we'll finished. It will be late. And it's too far for you to come."

She said, "Never mind. I'll come and stay with *makcik* until you get back. Every hour is precious. I don't know what will happen to them if you don't help. Even if you are angry with Yun Ming, you have known him for so long, you have always liked him. He's worked hard for you. Please have pity on him and Dahlan. They need your help now. If you tell those people to let them go, they will. I can be there about seven."

"It might be later than that."

"How much later?"

"Maybe eight or nine, I'm not sure. Even later."

"I'll stay with *makcik* until you come."

No one could say he deceived her. She was coming of her own free will. At nine o'clock. By ten o'clock she would be here. Definitely by eleven. She knew why she was coming. She knew what to expect. She wanted to come, otherwise she wouldn't come.

After stopping at a roadblock at the start of the Kuantan highway, manned by four men in civilian clothes armed with M-16s, the timber lorry with trailer wound round the corners of the road leading north out of the city. A line of cars followed it slowly. Occasionally one broke away with a screaming engine, overtaking a few vehicles before slipping back into the line. Sara kept her little Daihatsu in the queue all along the Karak highway. In the kilometre-long tunnel cut through solid rock, oncoming cars sped at her, their hazard lights blinking balefully. Emerging in the fading light of evening, she turned right and then sharply left and was instantly moving down a deserted country road overhung with branches from the virgin forest on the hillside. Although the sky in the distance was still flushed with the dying minutes of a glowing sunset, here the thick foliage of the whispering trees created a gloom over the surroundings.

In the half light she switched her headlights on, illuminating her path unevenly, descending rapidly for a few kilometres until the sound of a rushing stream became unmistakable. She was in a small open valley. A newly-built mosque loomed up on the left and a school building behind it. The road ahead of her became uncertain and disappeared into the jungle. On the right was an arched wooden bridge across the rapid flowing river. She parked her car and crossed the bridge. She was in the *dusun*. The imposing traditional wooden bungalow with spacious grounds ahead of her had a single light shining as she walked up to the porch.

The front door suddenly opened, and Panglima stood on the top step, his lips stretched in a slight smile. He was in a casual shirt and beige-coloured trousers. She stopped.

She said, "I thought you weren't going to be back until much later."

"Are you surprised?"

"I suppose not."

She entered the room and he bolted the door behind her. All the windows were closed to keep out flying night insects. From the wooden trestle supporting the roof a single bulb under a white conical shade hung from a cord, casting a yellow circle of light over the low centre table covered with a vinyl cloth of a gaudy flowered design and the glass vase of plastic flowers that stood on it. On the floor lay a half-opened newspaper in Jawi as if flung down in haste. Leading away from the sitting room, the dining area was in darkness with a poorly lit corridor behind.

She sat down in a wooden armchair outside the circular illumination that swung slowly with the white conical shade.

Panglima said, "You must be tired. Have you eaten?"

She said, "I'm not hungry. Anyway I have to get back soon. Where's *makcik*?"

He said, "I'll get you a glass of water. Maybe you like fresh lime?" He went into the dimly lit corridor and from there he said, "The power here is very low. We have to conserve. Mostly it's just one light and the refrigerator."

Through the trellis work along the top of the plank walls of the house a slight breeze came through. The sky was dark blue.

He came out and handed her a glass of lime juice, brushing her hand with his. His hand was wet. He stood over her.

He said, "Because of these two people you're in trouble. Why did you have to mix with them."

"Panglima, we have already lost time."

"Why, do you know what is going to happen to them?"

"They're going to send Yun Ming to the Northern Zone."

"Dahlan?"

"We were in a place somewhere near Kampung Puah. I heard they had taken Dahlan upriver. Panglima, you know so many people. Can you please ask them to help."

He bent down and pulled her up from her chair, and still holding her by both arms, pressed his lips hard against hers. She struggled, bumping into the centre table; the vase toppled and splintered. Still he held her by the wrists.

She said, "Where's *makcik*?"

His eyes were slits, his mouth tightened in a fixed smile. He said, "Don't worry, she's not here. She has gone to see our *cucu* in Kajang. She'll be there for a few days. Come now, Sara, you made me wait such a long time."

"I came to ask you for your help."

"Why do you worry about those two? They deserve everything they're going to get. Yun Ming has deserted his position, he has broken our laws. Dahlan has played with fire. Let them suffer."

She wrenched a hand free and reached for her bag. "I better go then."

"Do you want to save him?"

"That's why I came to you."

"That's not why you came, Sara." She was silent.

"Do you know why you came?"

"If you can't help to free Yun Ming, I will go."

"You came because you're *sundal*."

He held her tightly; she jerked her head one way and another to avoid his face. She felt his hardness and in a panic bit his lips. He screamed in pain, releasing her, and clapped his hand to his mouth which bled slightly. His slit eyes opened to the maximum, the gaze was intent though sightless. The corners of his mouth curled up and he thrust out a hand suddenly. Sara found herself staggering backward at great speed. Then she was on the floor holding her head which had struck the arm of a chair as she fell.

He said, "You're *sundal*, you make yourself cheap with a *kafir*, why were you acting like this with me."

She picked herself up, smoothing her shirt and jeans and walked without a word to the door. The image of Yun Ming and the first evening in the agriculture station in Sayong flashed across her mind; her eyes became moist.

Panglima was saying, "Never mind, I can forgive you. I can get the charge against you dropped."

She was shaking the door violently but it was locked; he had the key.

He said, "You have only caused me trouble, Sara. Do you know that?"

"I don't see how I caused you trouble. Let me go, please. Give me the keys."

"You talk freely, you dress freely, you only want to make people see you naked. You have caused me so much trouble, Sara, why don't you help me."

"What is there to help."

"You know how you can help me."

He was standing beyond the circle of light which swung about more sharply now. His legs and torso were illuminated; the upper part of his body was in the shade, so that he seemed headless.

She shuddered involuntarily and said, "I was a fool to come. Give me the key, please."

"You're wearing a Sarawak bead necklace. I've never seen you wear it before."

She touched it and let it fall back on the golden skin in the opening of her unbuttoned shirt.

"Did the Chinese give it to you? I can see from the way you look that he did."

"Panglima, I will not tell *makcik* what happened tonight. Please let me go quietly. If you don't, I will jump out of the window and bring the soldiers here."

"You think anyone will believe you. You're just a common *jalang*. You have already been arrested for *khalwat* and are awaiting trial."

She walked to a window and unbolted it. He made as if to come at her; she picked up a shard of the broken vase and held it defensively.

He said, "Yun Ming is locked in a classroom in a Sekolah Rendah two miles inside Kampung Puah. Rahim and his men are awaiting word from me to deliver him across the border if you do not return."

"Word from you?"

"Dahlan deserves everything he's been given so far. He is a traitor, he is *murtad*. He is in a hut in Teluk Udang where the villagers don't talk. He's luckier with us than he will be where he's going to."

"I don't understand what are you saying. Do you mean—"

He said, "They won't do anything without my orders." She said, "All along your loyalty for the nation—was it a sham?"

"No. True loyalty. I saw how the so-called modern values have led us to the situation we are now in. The people divided, so many religions, real *rojak*, partitioned not into two parts but many parts. We need a single set of values to keep us together."

"So you took away our rights and allowed others to become

power-mad. Why did you hide?" He said, "We are too few as yet. The people aren't ready—or interested. But we kept those in power off balance by what we did. Dahlan spoiled all that."

"What Dahlan did was selfless. He is our conscience."

He said, "Do you want to free him? And Yun Ming?" She stood rooted. He went up to her, looping one arm round her neck. His other hand moved slowly down her body. She gasped as he choked her. "Don't struggle, don't make a noise, whatever I do to you, or it will be worse for you—and them. Understand?" She was almost lifted off her feet.

He said, "Here is my telephone. It will be easy. One call to my people and those two will be free. If you do as I want. If you don't, be sure you will never see them again."

The arm tightened round her neck. "You agree? It will be easy for you, you're game for everyone, you know. You can smile so easily, so smile. When I let you go, smile."

He released her and turned her round. She was coughing, her face was red. He landed his fist on her temple and she staggered back a few steps. "I said smile, you're spoilt now, you should know. Show me how you like it. Yes! Yes! That's better."

He switched on the television and walked her into an inner room. In the subdued lighting he was shadow and dark substance. He switched on a bedside radio playing rock music softly. Was he the enemy she had feared all her life? She built in her head a small room in which she and Yun Ming were safe.

He poured something into two glasses and he handed her one. "Drink," he said.

She drank it in one gulp and her mind moved chaotically. He grasped at her with ferocity. His blows on her face and body left a tingling sensation after the pain. She cried sharply, "No!" when he thrust at her, but he held her in a vice, he was throttling her and shouting, "Smile, smile", and by some curious turn she answered him, taking with a savage relief, weeping, and screaming out against all the loneliness and guilt and the hatred and the sadness of her country and the memory of Yun Ming.

17

She entered the small room inside her head. Here phantoms played, brought alive by magic. The gaoler by her side was gone. She felt safe in her father's house; he was conducting a religious class. In the background, the sound of the quiet river which flowed past their house. The lovely notes of the *muezzin's* call without the aid of a loudspeaker wafted down and she sang in unison. Then the sun lured her out and she saw the tigers prowl. She saw her green thoughts floating down the brown river.

She shouted, "No one can accuse me of being rebellious or troublesome."

Gita said, "Lie still, Sara, you need to rest some more."

"I did everything I was told."

"Yes, Sara."

"I was cooperative."

"Yes."

"I was obedient."

"You were."

"I followed every word that was told to me."

"You did."

"To the letter. Ask them."

"Ask whom?"

"All of them. You will have to do the same, Gita. First they clamp a steel band round you. Then they strike it with a hammer, sending stinging pain to all parts of your body. They do not like inquiring thoughts. They only wish to assert their authority over you."

The door to her small room opened and she slipped back gratefully. The room was a dark box lined with black velvet. She couldn't see her gaoler, but he was there, just outside.

The steel band tightened. The pain was in her mind whenever she stopped the words seeking to rumble out by way of explanation, hearing only their grating sounds, sensing only their opaqueness, feeling only futility. The hardest thing was waiting—waiting to know whether the words uttered all around her were to be construed as official verdicts depriving her of all support, or whether they meant someone would take up her case again in the distant future, or whether her case was already concluded. To whom should she appeal when she did not know who her judge was or where he could be found?

Suddenly she noticed that the light which hurt her eyes came from the sun shining through the window. Sara floated to the window and saw the hedge of hibiscus in bloom again. She heard the greetings of passers-by and the honk of the ragman's three-wheeled motorcycle. From under the shade of the familiar rambutan tree an official adviser she recognised as Tseto bowed gravely to her. She shrank behind the curtain.

Why was it necessary for him to watch her here so openly with a tiger stalking by his side. Where were the other two?

From across a deep gorge, Safiah said, "What happened, *'dik*? Is it true?"

"What?"

"Never mind, I understand. No need to tell me. Come and sit down. Here's the good news, The charge against you has been dropped. Also against your friend. Now why are you crying? Is this something to be crying about? Your good *abah*, if he was alive, would be very happy. There now."

"Why are they still watching me then?"

"Where? Who?"

"Look out of the window and you'll see. They want to give me advice, they want to teach me. I felt so wretched that I cannot find the words to speak to them. They must be right, they feel so strongly. They strike the steel band round me, sending needles through my body. My hand twitches and I awake. Where's Gita?"

"She's not here."

"But I—spoke to her just now."

"She's staying with Dahlan's mother. *Adik*, listen to me, I must tell you some more."

She re-entered the little room in her head.

Gita said, "We found you unconscious in Panglima's house. Lucky thing we found you at all. We don't know what he intended to do with you. No, Sara, don't."

Sara sat on the bed, the tears coursing down her cheeks.

Gita said, "The doctor said you had been drugged. Panglima must have put something in your drink."

The sunlight faded, but straining her eyes she discerned the receding patches of blue sky between the leaves of the rambutan tree. The objects in the room, Gita, and in the background a figure who stood attentively in the shadow, became phantasmal. She was approaching the tunnel on the way to Durian Badak when Gita said, "Sara, no. Listen to me. Don't give up now when you've come through. Listen to me."

Dahlan came out of the shadow and stood in the light. He was wearing his lawyer's robes and he had on a wig. He carried a black pilot's bag and he was smiling.

He said, "Gita is right. Don't give up."

Sara said, "You're free."

He said, "Yes, at last. I saw what they were doing to me, I felt no pain. I saw all the details of my life, they were written on the waves of the sea. I saw Neelambigai waving. I saw the talks I gave, the hurt I caused. I was filled with despair. From the deeps I saw my Gita, she was calling to me, she consoled me. I'll go now."

She said again, "You're free."

He said, "You are, too."

Someone was shaking her violently. She staggered under the blows of a man's fists. Safiah said, "*Adik*, do you hear me? He was caught, they caught him, do you understand? There's no need to fear him any more."

"They caught Panglima."

"Who?"

Safiah said, "Omar and Gita. Yes, Omar. He's a good man, he brought you here. You know. They caught him."

"When did Omar come?"

"Two weeks ago. You were like, as if you were in a deep sleep. Gita helped him. It was strange to see how attentive he was to you."

Gita said, "I was desperate about Dahlan. I saw what they were doing to him. I was worried about you. I didn't know whom to ask for help. Every minute counted. I was trying to get Panglima. Yun Ming was caught, he couldn't help, so I asked Omar to take me to his house. We didn't know you were there. It was pitch dark when we arrived in the little valley. Our van bumped over the wooden bridge and we saw light through the slats of the windows of the house. But as we approached there were sounds of a struggle and cries and shouting. I didn't know what to do nor did Omar. Should we walk away, or should we knock? But we couldn't deny what we had heard. Finally, Omar coughed and walked up the steps and knocked on the door. Several times. Panglima's voice came out clear. 'People have gone to sleep, come back tomorrow.'

"Omar said, '*Pak*, it's me, Omar. There is an urgent matter, we need your help.'

"There was a long silence. Finally the door opened. He was in a *sarong* and sleeveless vest. The sweat on his face shone under the dim electric light. I caught the glint of a *parang* gripped by its haft and hidden behind the length of his right arm. Then we saw you. You shook your hair wildly. Your face was bruised, and you were whimpering. He tried to push you inside but he failed, while I tended to you I heard Omar say to him, '*Pak, what have you done? What shame have you brought on us all.*'

"Panglima said, 'She just *anak sundal*. Don't worry about her, Omar. It's a good thing you have thrown her out, she's just trash, trying to get favours from me.' Then he spoke sharply to you, 'Go inside.' But I held you and we did not move.

"Omar said to him, 'Panglima, I hope you will not stop me. I heard what you said—and I am very sad. I would never have believed it if I didn't hear it with my own ears. I have all along looked up to you for guidance and help. She did so also, I know.'

"Panglima said, 'She's not your wife anymore, so why do you care?'

"Omar said, 'True she is not my wife anymore but she's a human being. I'm going to take her from here. You have brought disgrace on us all. Believe me, now, your days of power are ended. I will tell them all. I hope you will not stop me now.'

"We both more or less dragged you away, Omar on one side of you, I on the other. We were at the door when Panglima spoke. He said, 'I was the one who got the charge against her and that Chinese dropped. If you go through with what you are saying, she'll be sorry, you also. I'll make sure they get what they deserve.'

"Omar said, 'Panglima, you have no more power in this. My *Penaung* called me and told me she had appealed to them. He said he and his fellow judges felt she deserved their consideration. He asked me if I would object if they let her go. They wanted to know how I felt. I know she was greatly attached to her father. Now he's gone, she has strayed because she has lacked his guidance. I do not want to spoil his memory. I told my *Penaung* I would agree with whatever they decided. They let her go, not you. You hear me, Panglima?'

"We went down the steps and reached the bridge and I said, 'If you come after us, Panglima, I will kill you.' But he did. I was frightened. We couldn't go any faster because we were holding and dragging you. The night sky was cloudy and the branches of the trees all around rose above us in a black, sighing shield. When he was almost upon us we turned around and backed away, warily. The *parang* still glinted behind the length of his hand. He was breathing heavily; he said, 'If you don't promise to keep silent about tonight, this woman will never see her husband again. I can get him free, it's up to you.' Sara, even as we backed away, my mind was in a turmoil because my last hope of helping Dahlan vanished the moment we entered Panglima's house. He said again, 'Give me your promise and he will be safe. I will just leave this zone and not come back. Here, I will make the call now.'

"Omar hesitated and looked at me. I think he saw even in the darkness the pleading in my eyes. He turned to Panglima and said, 'I promise. But you must call now.' Panglima stared at us and I know he was thinking whether to cut us down. 'When at last he turned away, I caught sight of the *parang* again. He went in and emerged a couple of minutes later, saying, 'All right. They will release him to you.'

"Omar said, 'Remember, if you have lied, I will tell all.'

"After we brought you home and placed you in Safiah's care, we drove like people possessed to Kampung Pauh where Dahlan was held. It broke my heart to see the state he was in. My God, Sara, it was pitiable. He was only a few hours in his hospital bed but he told me everything. When he passed away, I had no tears, just a numbness because I hadn't taken care of him enough, hadn't shown him enough how much I loved him for taking me out of the prison that my own life had been, for giving me a glimpse of a new world."

18

Sara opened her eyes to the pounding of rain on the roof of her father's house. Powerful gusts of wind repeatedly slammed into its walls, splattering rain water through the wooden-louvred windows onto the floorboards inside. Safiah said it was the heaviest downpour they had had for years. The coconut trees bent away from the wind's fury, their fronds flying wildly like the hair of demented creatures. Branches snapped and swished to the ground in loud soughs. Sara looked at the jagged bright blue streaks of lightning with fascination. They spat with unpredictable viciousness close to the house, and she caught in the split seconds of their illumination an inkling of a sphere of calm beyond.

In the evening the sky lightened. She stepped out of the house, the fresh air pricking her senses. The colour of the leaves different from bush to tree, and from tree to tree, in dazzling shades of green after the rain. The river, its waters swollen after the storm flowed more swiftly, making the *sampan* with a motor which operated as a ferry take a sharper angle against the current before coasting across down stream. Tiny figures got off at the opposite bank. The soft chug of the motor started again and the ferry turned round for its journey back. Sara walked up to the hedge of hibiscus where the flowers glistened blood-red; peering into one she saw again enticing, infinitely receding colour and stopped again, petrified. On a sprig nearby, a kingfisher perched unmoving, a brilliant assemblage of sky blue, dark brown and white and yellow beak. One evening she got on her bicycle and rode the path that ran alongside the river. Turning off she headed towards the *sawah* in the centre of which as on an island stood Safiah's homestead.

Safiah's husband said, "*Ala*, thank you. But why do you bring these things? You will only spoil the children. You're looking better now. Did my Haslina and Nur help you all right? Here, come and see where the rain has destroyed the bunds we made. Safiah and I will have to re-make them soon."

She was riding on the path alongside the river as if racing to meet the ferry boat approaching diagonally across the downward current. When she saw him, she turned round and pedalled fast. Why didn't her bicycle move? It was Vanar, holding on to it with gritted teeth. Lahab stood to one side with Tseto; they were smiling.

Yun Ming came up to her.

She said, "Ming, go back. Why have you come here? You don't know."

"I know."

She said, "I have no feeling, do you understand? Can you get that?"

It seemed he wasn't listening. He told her his father had passed away. "I couldn't call you, my line was cut. There was trouble in my area."

The image of the boar's head flashed through her mind, and she heard again the shotgun blast. She said, "I'm sorry to hear that, but you've got to understand. Look at those people. There."

He said, "Let me help you", placing his hands over hers holding the handlebars, and pulling the bicycle free. "Now, you look. Without their finery, outside those halls. Such ordinary, boring people." Vanar had a blank look on his face. She snatched her hands away in anger.

She said, "Keep away from me, don't touch me. Do you think you can trap me again as you did before?"

He was crowding her, just as Panglima did. Then he was saying something absurd about needing her. The house was in decay. Chris wanted everything sold and his share sent to him in Brisbane. He said, "That's okay, I don't want to live in the house. I've left my job, I've had enough. I'm lonely. Come with me to the Eastern Zone."

"You think if you insist on something for long enough you'll get it? Why are you all like that?"

She realised he was not listening. Just like that ape. Tears coursing down her cheeks, she stood on the pedals of her bicycle to burst away, but he held it till she spun around and fell.

The river took on a pallid hue. It seemed he wanted her no matter what she said. The people from the ferry boat watched, transfixed, the branches of the trees were motionless and no bird sang. Everything was strange as they walked awkwardly to the jetty for the journey across.

Vanar, Lahab and Tseto turned away.

A Note

The writing of this novel was suggested by an episode in Misa Melayu, *an 18th Century Malay literary and historical classic by* Raja Chulan Ibni Raja Hamid *(new edition, Penerbitan Pustaka Antara, 1962). The following is a summary of the episode:*

Once, Sultan Iskandar went upriver to Sayong on a pleasure trip. There was news that an elephant had been trapped in Padang Asam. After an expedition to Pachat where he saw it confined to an area so that it could be tamed, he returned to Sayong and was welcomed by Sri Maharaja Lela and all the warrior leaders of the districts around Sayong, Kota Lama and Talang, Padang Asam and Sungei Siput.

A story that was current in Sayong at about that time concerned a woman named Siti Sara, daughter of Lebai Hanap, a Tamil. She was married to a Tamil called Seri Raja Khan. After a while, they were divorced. Other men courted her but she did not wish to marry anyone from that area.

One suitor, named Abdullah, came from downstream and wanted to marry her. Siti Sara too wished to marry him. Seri Maharaja Lela gave his approval for the marriage. But when the men brought the *sireh* as a marriage offering it was rejected, because Seri Maharaja Lela had become infatuated with Siti Sara and wanted to marry her himself. Siti Sara refused.

Seri Maharaja Lela forcibly took her to his house and insisted that she marry him, for he was the Penghulu of the district. Siti Sara steadfastly refused. She loved Abdullah and Abdullah still wanted to marry her.

Abdullah again asked Seri Maharaja Lela for his permission, but was again refused. Abdullah then took his suit to Raja Kechil Besar who had once been a pupil of Imam Panjang, Abdullah's father. Raja Kechil Besar brought the matter up with Seri Maharaja Lela and Raja Bijaya Dewa. But however much he pleaded with them on Abdullah's behalf, they still refused to approve the betrothal.

Since all hope was lost, Abdullah and Siti Sara came together in love. Seri Maharaja Lela was angry when he heard this. He felt humiliated that Siti Sara did not want him. He offered her to the Sultan as a slave and the Sultan accepted her.

Later, the Sultan sailed downstream and when he reached Pachat he stopped there to wait until the elephant had been tamed.

Glossary
(by Adibah Amin)

A

abang older brother; also used to address husbands

B

baju kurung straight-cut traditional Malay women's blouse

baju/baju Melayu traditional Malay shirt

balai raya community hall

balik kampung return to one's village

bubur rice porridge

bumiputra 'sons of the soil', political term for Malays

C

ceramah lecture, talk

cucu grandchild

D

dewan large hall

dusun fruit orchard

G

gamelan orchestra of gongs, xylophones, drums, common to Malaysia and Indonesia

gasing tops, game of tops

H

halal allowed by Islam

halaman courtyard

haram forbidden by Islam

hukum hudud Islamic Penal Code

I

Imam Islamic prayer leader

intan diamond (used as a term of endearment)

J

jalang bitch (derogatory)

janggut beard (used as a derogatory nickname)

jubah long garment for Muslim women

K

kafir non-believer in Islam

kapitan 'Captain', title for head of a Chinese community

khalwat Sharia offence of 'close proximity' between two unmarried and unrelated persons of the opposite sex

khianat religious treachery

kendi a small water container with a spout and handle

kopiah Islamic skull cap

L

lebai respectful way of calling a pious man/religious teacher

lorong lane

M

macam api dalam sekam like fire in straw (spreads easily)

madrasah Islamic school

maghrib time for Islamic sunset prayers

Masa 'tu hebat, kak. Saya masuk operasi jolok manggis. Banyak dapat It was great, sis. I joined Operation Bring Down Mangosteens [killing Indians]. We got lots of them.

Merdeka Independence

muezzin chosen person at a mosque leading and reciting the call to prayer

muhibah goodwill (often inter-racial goodwill)

murtad apostasy

P

Panglima General

penaung protector/patron (here more a dictator)

penghulu Malay village headman

penyakit merah a type of *padi* infestation

politik suku agama suku politics and religion must be kept separate

R

relong measurement of area

rezeki divinely allotted portion in life

rumah tumpangan small hotel

S

sambal tumis hot spicy dish

sawah padi field

sembah obeisance

sireh betel leaf

sundal/anak sundal whore

T

Tada, tada. Ada orang, yo. Jaga baik-baik. No room, no room! There are people here. Be very careful.

tok guru respectful way of calling a religious teacher

tudung Muslim women's head covering

U

ulama Islamic religious teachers

Y

Yang di-Pertua president of an association

Z

zina illicit sex